READ ALOUD PLAYS:
The
Middle Ages

by Jeannette Sanderson

SCHOLASTIC
PROFESSIONAL BOOKS

NEW YORK • TORONTO • LONDON • AUCKLAND • SYDNEY
MEXICO CITY • NEW DELHI • HONG KONG

Dedicated to Glenn, Catie, and Nolan

ACKNOWLEDGMENTS

*Thanks to Virginia Dooley, Jean Greenough,
Lisa Hall, and the staff of the Field Library in Peekskill, New York,
for their contributions to this book.*

Cover design by Laura Boragara
Interior design by Solutions by Design, Inc.
Interior illustrations by Mona Mark

ISBN 0-590-76993-6

Table of Contents

Introduction

Welcome to the Middle Ages. The eight plays in this book are designed to bring you and your students into the exciting period between ancient and modern history that spanned the one thousand years from about 500 to 1500 A.D.

The plays have a variety of sources. Six of them (*The Song of Roland, Bisclavret, Robin Hood Helps a Sorrowful Knight, The Divided Horse Blanket, Patient Griselda,* and *Sir Gawain and the Green Knight*) are adaptations of stories told during the Middle Ages. *The Making of the Magna Carta* is a retelling of the events that led to the creation of one of the most important documents in history. And *Joan of Arc* is a dramatic account of the life of one of the most famous persons who lived during the Middle Ages. The plays are in rough chronological order, based on when the events in each actually or imaginatively took place.

Each play is followed by a teaching guide to help you and your students get the most out of your reading. The teaching guides are divided into two sections: Background and Making Connections.

The first section, Background, enhances your class's reading and understanding of the play with additional information about the play's subject and, if applicable, the original story's author. It also contains Words to Know, a list of words from the play whose meaning your students should know to help them get the most out of their reading.

Making Connections contains questions to use as discussion starters or writing prompts and extension activities to help students further appreciate the play, its subject, and the time period. The cross-curricular activities emphasize discussion,

writing, research, and cooperative learning. The Further Reading sections feature books which can be used to learn more about the subject of a particular play or as a stepping stone for research into the time period.

Prepare for the reading of each play by asking what, if anything, students already know about its subject. Then review the special vocabulary. Share the background information from the teaching guide with students. If time allows, you may want to assign related background reading.

The plays can be read aloud or acted. Most plays have a large number of characters so that many students can have a chance to read or perform. The majority of roles are male. Point this out to students. Then, after discussing what this says about medieval society, tell students that any student can play any role, regardless of gender. Encourage all students to participate in the reading or acting of the plays.

Readings can be done just with your class or can be shared with other classes. After rehearsing the play, you might consider performing it for the school, parents, or community.

Enjoy!

The Song of Roland

A French Epic

Characters (in order of appearance):

NARRATOR

KING MARSILE: pagan ruler of Spain

BLANCANDRIN: one of King Marsile's knights

PAGANS: King Marsile's men

KING CHARLES: Charlemagne, King of the Franks

FRANKS: Charles' men

ROLAND: Charles' brave warrior nephew

GANELON: Roland's stepfather

DUKE NAIMES: one of Charles' counselors

AELROTH: one of King Marsile's men

OLIVER: one of Charles' counts, Roland's friend

ARCHBISHOP TURPIN: one of Charles' men

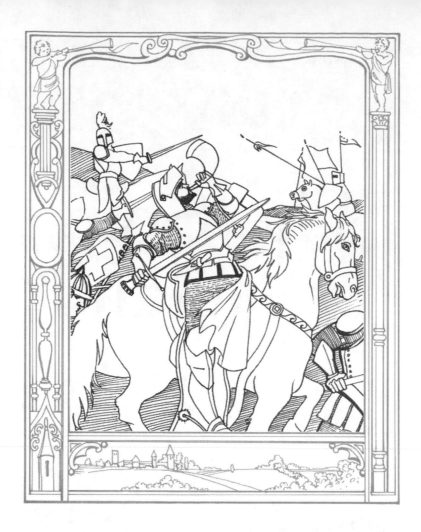

ꙮ ACT I ꙮ

SCENE 1:

Late summer, 778 A.D.
Saragossa, Spain.

NARRATOR: King Charles had been in Spain for seven years. During that time, he conquered every castle and city except Saragossa. That city on a hill, where King Marsile made his home, was Charles's next target. King Marsile knew that.

KING MARSILE: Charles has come to this country to destroy us. My army cannot match his in battle. Tell me, counselors, how to avoid death and shame.

NARRATOR: There was a long silence. Then one of Marsile's wisest men spoke.

BLANCANDRIN: You are not yet defeated, my king. Promise Charles your friendship and service. Offer him great riches. Tell him you will follow him to France at Michaelmas and receive the Christian faith there. Tell him you will send hostages to guarantee it.

NARRATOR: The group of pagans gasped.

BLANCANDRIN: Wait. Then Charles will return to France. He will hold a great festival in expectation of your arrival. But you will not come.

PAGANS: But what of the hostages?

BLANCANDRIN: Charles will surely have them beheaded. But better for them to lose their heads than for us to lose our fair land of Spain.

KING MARSILE: You speak wisely, Blancandrin. Go to King Charles with this offer. Take my finest men, and carry olive branches in your hands.

6

NARRATOR: Blancandrin did as the king ordered.

SCENE 2:

The following day. At King Charles' camp at Cordoba.

NARRATOR: King Charles sat in a garden with some of his most loyal vassals. Blancandrin and his men arrived on horseback, bearing olive branches.

BLANCANDRIN (*dismounting*)**:** We greet you with love and goodwill. King Marsile has a message for you.

KING CHARLES: What is it?

BLANCANDRIN: My king wishes to convert to Christianity and to give you a large portion of his wealth.

NARRATOR: King Charles bowed his head to think and pray.

BLANCANDRIN: You have been in this country a long time. There is nothing left to conquer. If you go back to France, my king promises to follow you there at Michaelmas.

KING CHARLES (*looking up*)**:** King Marsile is my sworn enemy. How do I know you tell the truth?

BLANCANDRIN: He offers you hostages. I will even send my own son.

KING CHARLES (*hopeful*)**:** Your king might yet be saved.

NARRATOR: The king rose and walked over to a pine tree. He called for his barons to join him.

KING CHARLES: My lord barons, I ask your guidance. You have heard King Marsile's message. Am I to believe him?

NARRATOR: The king looked at his men. His eyes settled on his nephew, Roland.

ROLAND: If you believe Marsile you will regret it. Do you remember the last time he sent you pagans with olive branches? He had your return messengers beheaded!

NARRATOR: King Charles and his men nodded, remembering.

ROLAND: My king, wage war as you set out to do. Saragossa will soon be yours.

NARRATOR: The king bowed his head in thought. Then Roland's step-father spoke to the king.

GANELON: If King Marsile wishes to surrender, we should listen with open ears. This war has lasted long enough.

DUKE NAIMES: There is sense in Count Ganelon's words. You have already defeated King Marsile by taking all his castles and cities, save one. It would be a sin to proceed since he asks for your mercy, especially since he offers hostages as assurance.

FRANKS: The duke has spoken well.

NARRATOR: All nodded, save Roland.

KING CHARLES: Then we shall accept Marsile's proposal and stop the war. Whom shall we send to him with word of our acceptance?

ROLAND: Although I disagree with your decision, as your nephew and servant, I am prepared to go.

KING CHARLES: No, I want you here with me. Someone else must go.

ROLAND: Then I nominate Ganelon.

FRANKS: He is well suited for the job.

NARRATOR: Ganelon looked at Roland with unhidden anger.

GANELON: You fool! If God grants that I return from Saragossa, I will cause you trouble for the rest of your life.

KING CHARLES: Come forth, Ganelon. You have been nominated by the Franks.

GANELON: This is Roland's doing. If I live, I will never lose any love for him.

KING CHARLES: You have an evil disposition, Ganelon, but still you shall go. It is my command.

NARRATOR: Ganelon quickly turned away. He went to his tent and donned his armor. He mounted his war horse and rode to where Blancandrin and the others awaited him. Then they rode off to Saragossa, with Ganelon clearly miserable.

GANELON (*to himself*): Roland will yet be shamed by his action! (*to Blancandrin*) Roland loves the emperor. For him he will conquer lands from here to the Orient.

BLANCANDRIN: I have heard of Roland's many conquests. He is a brave and dangerous man.

NARRATOR: Ganelon thought for a few moments. Then he smiled to himself.

GANELON: If anyone were to kill Roland, we would all have peace.

NARRATOR: Blancandrin smiled as he looked at Ganelon.

BLANCANDRIN: I sense that you do not like Roland.

NARRATOR: Ganelon did not have to say a word. The hatred on his face spoke for him.

BLANCANDRIN: Do you also want peace?

GANELON: I do.

BLANCANDRIN: Then let us bring about the death of Roland.

SCENE 3:
Late that day. Back at Saragossa.

NARRATOR: Upon his return, Blancandrin went straight to see King Marsile. He brought Ganelon with him.

BLANCANDRIN: We carried your message to Charles, my lord. He has sent Count Ganelon, one of his own noble barons, to show that he accepts your proposal.

NARRATOR: Count Ganelon nodded to the king.

KING MARSILE: And now I must send him the riches I promised, along with twenty hostages. (*He sighed.*) Tell me, Count Ganelon. Will Charles ever tire of waging war?

GANELON (*shaking his head*): Never.

KING MARSILE (*outraged*): Perhaps we should continue this fight, and start by beheading this noble Frankish baron!

BLANCANDRIN: Wait, my lord. Count Ganelon also wants this war to end. He has given me his word he will help our cause.

KING MARSILE (*to Ganelon*): How can you help us?

GANELON: Charles will never tire of waging war as long as his nephew Roland lives. There is no man like Roland, and Charles fears nothing as long as Roland is alive.

KING MARSILE: Then we must bring about Roland's death, but how?

GANELON: Do as you said you would. Give the king the great wealth and hostages you promised. Tell him again that you will follow him to France and become a Christian. The king will then leave.

KING MARSILE: Where will Roland be?

GANELON: I will see to it that he is

READ ALOUD PLAYS: THE SONG OF ROLAND
Scholastic Professional Books, 1998

stationed in the rearguard of the king's army. You can attack the rearguard when it is in one of the narrow passes.

NARRATOR: The king nodded.

GANELON: You must send one hundred thousand of your men to fight against Roland. He is very brave. There will be many losses amongst your men, but Roland will not escape.

NARRATOR: King Marsile kissed Ganelon. He gave him a gold, jewel-encrusted sword and fine necklaces for his wife. Then, in accordance with his false agreement, he had seven hundred camels loaded with gold and silver for King Charles. He gathered twenty of his best young men for hostages.

KING MARSILE: Present this treasure and these hostages to King Charles along with my word that I will follow him to France at Michaelmas. Then have Roland appointed to the rearguard, where I shall engage him in mortal combat.

GANELON: I will do as you ask. Now I must be going, I have stayed too long.

NARRATOR: Ganelon climbed onto his great horse and, leading the train of camels and hostages, rode away.

❧ ACT II ❧

SCENE 1:
The following day. Back at King Charles' camp.

NARRATOR: Count Ganelon arrived back at camp the next day at dawn. King Charles was waiting for him.

GANELON: My mighty king, I bring you much from King Marsile: great riches, twenty hostages, and his word that he will follow you into France and receive the faith you hold.

KING CHARLES (*lowering his head*): Thanks be to God. (*looking at Ganelon*) You have done well, Count Ganelon. Your reward will be great.

NARRATOR: Count Ganelon bowed his head to hide his deceitful eyes.

KING CHARLES (*to his men*): Sound the bugles! We shall break camp and return to France!

NARRATOR: A thousand bugles were sounded, and the Franks loaded their pack horses.

KING CHARLES: Lord barons, there are many narrow passes in these mountains we must cross. We need a strong vanguard and rearguard. Who shall lead these detachments?

GANELON: I nominate my stepson to lead your rearguard. He is your most valiant man.

ROLAND: I know not your reasons, Ganelon, but I accept your nomination. I will protect my king in the rearguard, I will not let him down.

KING CHARLES: Fair nephew, I shall give you half my army for your task.

ROLAND: Rightful emperor, I need only twenty thousand of your most fearless Franks. We shall protect you to the end. You need fear no one in my lifetime.

NARRATOR: King Charles lowered his head. He stroked his beard and twisted his mustache. Something did not feel right, and tears fell from his eyes.

KING CHARLES (*looking up*): Take what you need, nephew. And may God be with you.

NARRATOR: Roland rounded up his men. Among them was Oliver, his companion and one of Charles's best men. They fell to

the rear as Charles and the others rode on.

KING CHARLES: Something weighs heavily on my mind.

DUKE NAIMES: What is it?

KING CHARLES: I am remembering a dream I had last night. A man came and broke my lance.

DUKE NAIMES: Who was the man?

NARRATOR: Tears fell down the king's cheeks.

KING CHARLES: It was Ganelon, who nominated my nephew to the rearguard. I do not know what I would do if I lost Roland!

NARRATOR: The king and his men rode on in silence with a deep feeling of dread for Roland.

SCENE 2:
August 15, 778. At the pass at Roncesvalles.

NARRATOR: Roland and his men were in the pass at Roncesvalles when they heard the noise of a thousand pagan's trumpets.

OLIVER: Lord, companion, I think we may have a battle.

ROLAND: And may God grant it to us. We will serve our king and prove that the pagans are wrong, and the Christians are right. And we shall fight so that no one will ever sing a shameful song about us.

NARRATOR: Suddenly, a huge army of pagans came into view.

OLIVER: Ganelon has betrayed us! I have never seen so many pagans. There are so many of them and so few of us. Companion Roland, blow your horn. Let Charles know he and the army should turn back.

ROLAND: I will not blow my horn in

cowardice and lose my good name.

OLIVER: Blow your horn! Charles will hear it and turn the army around.

ROLAND: Heaven forbid that any man alive should say that pagans made me blow my horn to summon help.

OLIVER: I see no shame in calling for help. Their army is vast, and we have but a tiny company of men.

ROLAND: The Franks are brave. They will strike courageously. I shall strike thousands of blows with Durendal, my good sword.

NARRATOR: The two men watched the huge army hurtle towards them on horseback.

OLIVER: If Charles were here, we would suffer no harm. But you refuse to blow your horn, and the rearguard is in great trouble. (*He shakes his head mournfully.*) Those who are part of this rearguard shall never form another.

ROLAND (*angry*): Do not speak such words! There is not a coward among our twenty thousand men. I swear to you, Oliver, all of those pagans are condemned to die.

NARRATOR: Roland called to Archbishop Turpin to bless the Franks before the battle. Then Roland shouted to his men.

ROLAND: My lord barons, be brave! These pagans are heading for great slaughter!

NARRATOR: Aelroth, who led the pagans, mocked Roland.

AELROTH: Foolish Franks! He who should have protected you has betrayed you. The king is a fool to have left you in this pass.

NARRATOR: On hearing those words, Roland charged Aelroth and struck him dead.

ROLAND: The first blow is ours!

10

NARRATOR: Within moments, the enemies were locked in heated battle.

SCENE 3:

Later that day. At Roncesvalles.

NARRATOR: The battle continued. The dead of both armies littered the battlefield. But Roland's army was clearly superior; so far, it had killed one hundred thousand pagans.

ARCHBISHOP TURPIN: No one on earth could have braver men than we.

NARRATOR: King Marsile arrived with hundreds of thousands of reinforcements. The Franks looked pleadingly to Archbishop Turpin, their spiritual leader.

ARCHBISHOP TURPIN: Be not afraid, my lords. We will soon be in holy paradise. And because we died fighting, no one will sing a shameful song of us.

NARRATOR: The Franks fought on. Many of them fell, but they felled even more pagans. King Marsile could not believe his eyes.

KING MARSILE: Mighty land of France, Mohammed curse you! Your men are bolder than all the others!

NARRATOR: As bold and brave as the Franks were, they could not last forever against Marsile's reinforcements. Soon, there were only a handful of Charles's men left alive.

ROLAND (*to Oliver*): Our battle is fierce. I shall sound the horn and King Charles will hear it.

OLIVER: Do not speak of that to me. It is too late now. If you had heeded me earlier, my lord would be here now. We should have fought this battle and won it. Now Franks are dead because of your recklessness.

NARRATOR: The Archbishop heard the two friends quarreling and rode over to them.

ARCHBISHOP TURPIN: Lord Roland and Lord Oliver, I beg you, do not argue.

NARRATOR: Roland looked at his horn.

ARCHBISHOP TURPIN: Blow the horn, Roland. It will not save us, but when the king hears it, he will return and avenge our deaths. He will see to it that we are buried on sacred ground.

ROLAND: Lord, you speak well.

NARRATOR: Roland put the horn to his lips. He blew so hard that his temple burst. Blood gushed from his nose, his mouth, even his ears. But the sound was long and clear.

SCENE 4:

At the same time. Near the front of King Charles's army.

NARRATOR: The sound of Roland's horn traveled far. The king heard it.

KING CHARLES (*upset*): I hear Roland's horn. He must be in battle.

GANELON: There is no battle. Roland would blow his horn if he saw a hare.

NARRATOR: The king heard the horn again.

KING CHARLES: The sound is long and drawn out. Roland is surely in battle.

GANELON: There is no battle. Who would dare attack Roland the brave? Do not …

DUKE NAIMES (*interrupting*): Roland is in battle, my lord. And he who wants you to believe otherwise has betrayed him.

NARRATOR: The king called his servants. He pointed to Ganelon.

KING CHARLES: Seize this traitor! Guard

him well. He has betrayed my household!

DUKE NAIMES: My lord, hear the distress cry which Roland sends. You must ride to the aid of your noble household.

NARRATOR: The king had his trumpets sounded for war. The Franks armed themselves and mounted their war horses. Then Charles led his huge army back to Roncesvalles.

❧ ACT III ❧

SCENE 1:

A short while later. Back at Roncesvalles.

NARRATOR: Roland, Oliver, and Archbishop Turpin were all that remained of the Frankish rearguard. Still, they fought on.

ROLAND: When Charles, my lord, comes to this field, he will not fail to bless us. For every one of us, he will find fifteen pagans dead. Come, let us fight to the end.

OLIVER: A curse on the slowest man!

NARRATOR: Shortly thereafter, Oliver suffered a mortal blow. He called to Roland with his last breaths.

OLIVER: Lord companion, come and fight by my side. We shall part in great sorrow this day.

NARRATOR: When Roland reached Oliver, he was dead.

ROLAND: Lord companion, now that you are dead, it grieves me to remain alive.

NARRATOR: Overcome with grief and rage, Roland knocked twenty pagans down dead. Archbishop Turpin killed five. Then the air was shattered with the sound of sixty thousand French bugles blowing.

ROLAND: Charles, who will avenge us, is on his way back!

ARCHBISHOP TURPIN: Let us strike well to the end!

PAGANS: Their emperor is returning! How sad that we were ever born. Let us cast our spears and arrows at these Franks and flee!

NARRATOR: The pagans surrounded Roland and the Archbishop. They hurled their weapons and fled. The archbishop was mortally wounded. Roland knelt beside him.

ROLAND: Oh, noble man. May your soul know no suffering and find the gates of paradise wide open!

NARRATOR: Roland knew that his death was also near. He had suffered no wounds from the enemy, but the injury from blowing his horn was killing him. He lay down on the green grass beneath a pine tree and turned his head towards Spain, the land of the enemy.

ROLAND: Oh, God, I confess my sins, protect my soul from evil.

NARRATOR: Roland held out his hand and died.

SCENE 2:

A short while later. At Roncesvalles.

NARRATOR: King Charles cried out in agony when he reached Roncesvalles. The entire earth was covered with the dead bodies of Franks and pagans.

KING CHARLES: Where are you, fair nephew? Where are all my great men?

NARRATOR: There was no sound, save that of tens of thousands of knights and barons weeping at the sight of their fallen sons, brothers, fathers, and friends.

12

KING CHARLES: What sorrow I was not here when the battle began.

DUKE NAIMES: Look, lord. In the distance. It is the pagan army running away. Go after them. Avenge our sorrow.

KING CHARLES: One thousand men will remain here and guard our dead. Let us do what we must do.

NARRATOR: The king and his great army rode after the pagans. When darkness began to fall, King Charles got off his horse and knelt on the ground.

KING CHARLES: Dear God, hold back the night so that I may avenge the deaths of my men.

NARRATOR: An angel appeared and told King Charles to ride on, that the sun would remain where it was. Soon Charles met the fleeing pagans in battle. Those he and his men did not slay were driven to the River Ebro and drowned. The sun did not set until the battle was over.

SCENE 3:

The following day. At Roncesvalles.

NARRATOR: Charles and his men returned to Roncesvalles early the next morning.

KING CHARLES: Lords, let me go ahead. I would like to find my nephew.

NARRATOR: The king walked through the field, past the corpses of so many of his men. When he found Roland beneath the pine tree, he fainted.

KING CHARLES (*coming to*)**:** Beloved Roland, may God have mercy on you. You once said that if you ever died on foreign soil, your head would be turned towards the enemy's land. You were, indeed, a conqueror until the end.

NARRATOR: King Charles sobbed and tugged at his beard.

KING CHARLES: I will know sorrow for the rest of my days.

DUKE NAIMES: Lord, do not display such bitter grief. Search the field for our men so that we may take them to a proper place for burial.

NARRATOR: King Charles rose and ordered the field searched for his men, so that they could be buried on hallowed ground. Then he returned to France, where he had Roland's stepfather tried for treason. Ganelon was found guilty and died a terrible death: After watching thirty of his kinsmen hanged, he was drawn and quartered.

THE END

The Song of Roland

Teaching Guide

Background

About the Play

This play is based on the poem *The Song of Roland*, which was written about 1100 A.D. by an unknown French author. This story, about the greatest of the legendary knights to serve Charlemagne, is the oldest existing epic poem in French. There are several surviving manuscripts, all of which appear to be derived from a lost original.

The poem probably began as a popular song about a bloody battle fought in 778 A.D. when Charlemagne, King of the Franks, was returning from a military expedition to Spain. During the journey home, the rearguard of his army was ambushed and annihilated by a mountain people called Basques in

---

WORDS TO KNOW

baron: a nobleman; generally the tenant-in-chief of a property

count: a nobleman in rank above a baron

duke: a nobleman of highest rank

Franks: the people of the former kingdom that contained what is now Belgium, France, Luxembourg, the Netherlands, and part of West Germany

knight: a nobleman and soldier

lance: a steel-tipped spear carried by mounted knights

Michaelmas: the feast of St. Michael the Archangel, celebrated September 29

pagan: one who has no religion or is not a Christian

rearguard: a military detachment detailed to bring up and protect the rear of the main body

vanguard: the troops moving at the head of an army

vassal: a servant who has sworn allegiance to an overlord

Roncesvalles, a valley in the Pyrenees. Roland, Count of the Marches of Brittany, was the chief hero celebrated in these songs.

By the time it was written down, the legend lost much of its resemblance to actual events. For example, although it was the Basques who had attacked Charlemagne's rearguard, in the story it became the Saracens, Muslims who had invaded parts of the Christian world from the 600s to the 1000s. This change allowed the author to raise the clash to one between Christians and pagans. The author also took other liberties with history, including turning Charles into an old man (he was actually just 36 at the time of the Roncesvalles incident) and making Roland Charles' nephew, which he was not.

About Charlemagne: Charlemagne (742-814), the great emperor, referred to as King Charles in *The Song of Roland,* was the most famous ruler in the Middle Ages. Also known as Charles the Great or Charles I, Charlemagne was King of the Franks from 768-814 and emperor of the West from 800-814. Charlemagne conquered much of western Europe and united it under a great empire. During his rule, he established feudalism as the basic political and military system of Europe; he increased the food supply; stimulated trade; supported justice and good government; and improved education and culture, among other things. Although his strong empire fell apart after his death in 814, the reforms and improvements he implemented had lasting effects on European life.

About Feudalism: Feudalism was the system of political organization in much of Europe from the ninth to about the fifteenth centuries. Simply put, this system was based on an exchange of promises between the owners of the land and their tenants. The power hierarchy was shaped like a pyramid with the king, who owned all the land, on top. Under

him were the greatest barons and the bishops. These crown tenants, as they were called because they held their lands on a grant from the crown, usually held great amounts of land, and, as a result, owed much to their lord, the king. To help ease the burden of their debt, they divided their land up among their own vassals, and so on down to the base of the pyramid, which was supported by the peasants, both free and not.

In exchange for the lord's grants of land and promises of protection, vassals pledged their loyalty, paid certain fees, and gave a specified amount of goods and services. Among these services was the tenant's promise to fight for the lord when called on to do so. Tenants who did not wish to fight could pay a fee called *scutage,* meaning "shield money," that would allow the lord to hire professional fighting men to take his place.

Making Connections

Responding to the Play

Making sacrifices: Early in the play, Blancandrin says the pagans should send hostages to Charles. Ask students if they agree with Blancandrin's opinion that it is "Better for them to lose their heads than for us to lose our fair land of Spain"? Why or why not? What do they think they would be willing to sacrifice for their country?

War or peace? Ask students to imagine themselves in King Charles's shoes when Blancandrin presented King Marsile's proposal. Would they have chosen war or peace? Why?

A sixth sense? Before the attack at Roncesvalles, King Charles had a premonition that something would happen to Roland. On what was this premonition based? Do you think he should have done something about this hunch? Ask students if they have ever had a

premonition. Should people pay attention to premonitions? Why or why not?

Courage or foolishness? Oliver wanted Roland to use his horn to summon Charles's help. Roland thought it would be shameful to call for help. Ask students what they think. Was Roland being brave or foolish in refusing to call for help? What do students think they would have done in the same situation? Discuss with students what virtues, such as courage, bravery, honesty, and loyalty, seem to be most important in *The Song of Roland*.

Extension Activities

Telling tall tales: Cut a story from the local newspaper about an interesting and exciting recent event. It could be the high school basketball team's amazing comeback win, the rescue of a cat up a tree, or a foiled robbery attempt. (You might want to ask each student to find and bring in one such article, which you can sort through to find one for use with the whole class.) Copy and share this article with the class. Then ask each student to write and illustrate a one-page tall tale that somehow gets its start from the news article. Remind students that *The Song of Roland* is based on an actual event, but after years of retelling, it became so embellished that it possesses just a grain of historical accuracy.

Two sides of the story: Ask students to think about the viewpoint of *The Song of Roland*. Ask them to think about how—if they had existed at the time—newspapers of France and Spain might have differed in their account of the battle at Roncesvalles. Then divide the class in half. Ask one half to compose a newspaper article about the battle from the viewpoint of the Franks, the other half to compose one from the viewpoint of the Spaniards. Read the articles aloud. Ask students how they compare and contrast. Ask students if they think newspapers today contain biases, and, if so,

what that says about how they should be read.

Windows to history: Tell students that many events of the Middle Ages were illustrated in the stained glass windows of cathedrals built at the time. Ask students if they have seen stained glass windows; if so, ask them to describe them to the class. If possible, show the class examples from books. Then have each student "make" a tracing paper stained glass window based on *The Song of Roland*. After they choose the scene they wish to record, have them outline it in pencil. Then suggest that they use black markers for the outlines and colored markers for the insides. When these "windows" are completed, you might want to frame them with heavy construction paper and hang them on windows.

The Three Estates (Reproducible #1): Save this reproducible (page 17) for use throughout this book. After reading the last play, you may want to discuss why the distribution of characters does not reflect the entire population of the Middle Ages. Point out that, although most people were peasants, there was very little written about them, since most peasants could neither read nor write. For this play, ask students to place the names of the main characters—King Charles, Roland, Oliver, and Archbishop Turpin—in their proper estates.

Further Reading

For Students:
The Middle Ages (History of Everyday Things series) by Giovanni Caselli (Peter Bedrick Books 1993).

For Teachers:
The Song of Roland by Glyn Burgess (Penguin 1970).

The Knight in History by Frances Gies (Harper 1984).

Medieval Europe: A Short History by C. Warren Hollister (Knopf 1982).

Name _____

The Three Estates

In the Middle Ages there were three classes, or "estates," of people. These were the churchmen and women, the nobles, and ordinary people. Although the people of the church and the ruling class were very powerful, they only made up a small portion of the population. Most of the population—80 to 90 percent—was made up of ordinary people. Place the names of the main characters from the play in their proper estates.

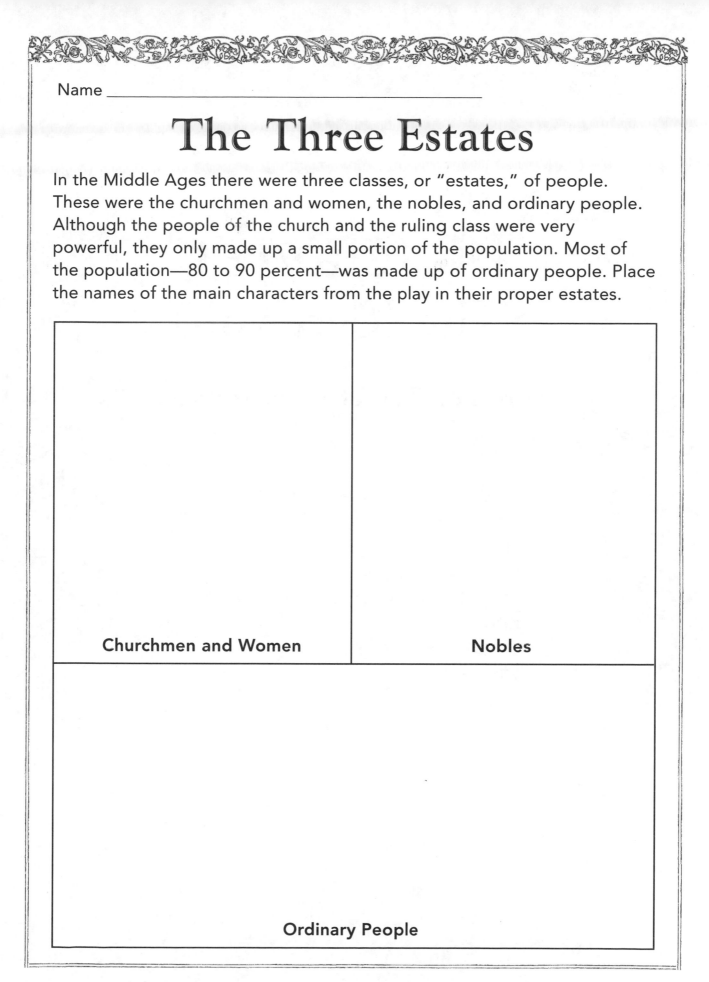

Churchmen and Women

Nobles

Ordinary People

Bisclavret (The Werewolf)

From the Lais of Marie de France

Characters (in order of appearance):

NARRATOR

BISCLAVRET

WIFE: Bisclavret's wife

KNIGHT: a nobleman who loves Bisclavret's wife

KING

COURTIERS 1-3: members of the king's court

WISE MAN

⚜ ACT I ⚜

SCENE 1:

Early Middle Ages. At a nobleman's home in Brittany, France.

NARRATOR: There once was a fine, handsome knight who was loved by all. We shall call him Bisclavret. This knight was married to a pretty woman, whom he loved very much. She loved him, as well, but something was troubling her.

BISCLAVRET: My lovely wife, why are you so unhappy?

WIFE: My lord and dear love, something is troubling me. I would ask you about it, if I dared.

BISCLAVRET: My lady, go ahead and ask!

There's nothing you could want to know that, if I knew the answer, I wouldn't tell you.

WIFE: My lord, on the days when you go away from me, I am in such a state—so sad at heart, so afraid I'll lose you—that I could die.

NARRATOR: Each week Bisclavret disappeared for three whole days. Neither his wife nor his men knew what happened to him or where he went.

WIFE: Please tell me where you go, what you do. Is there another woman?

BISCLAVRET: There is no other woman. But, my dear, you must not ask me about this. Harm will come to me if I answer your questions.

WIFE: How will you be harmed by being honest with your wife?

BISCLAVRET: If I told you the truth, I would lose your love. And perhaps even my very self.

NARRATOR: Bisclavret had hoped that that was the end of the discussion, but his wife would not stop questioning him.

WIFE: My dear, I love you so much. It breaks my heart that you should keep something from me.

BISCLAVRET: You do not really want to know…

WIFE (interrupting): But I do.

BISCLAVRET (sighing): All right. If you must know… (pausing) I become a werewolf.

NARRATOR: The wife was speechless. After several long moments she regained her composure.

WIFE: A werewolf?

BISCLAVRET (sad): Yes. Now you know.

WIFE: But what do you do?

BISCLAVRET: I go off into the great forest, in the thickest part of the woods, and I live on the prey I hunt down.

NARRATOR: The wife was curious, despite her fear and revulsion.

WIFE: Do you wear your clothes when you are a werewolf?

BISCLARVET (hanging his head): Wife, I go stark naked.

WIFE: Then where are your clothes?

BISCLAVRET: That I will not tell you, for if I were to lose them, I would stay a werewolf forever.

NARRATOR: The wife tried to hide her excitement at learning this piece of information.

WIFE (reaching for Bisclavret's hand): My lord, I love you more than all the world.

You must not hide anything from me.

BISCLAVRET: But I do not want the hiding place to be known. It is too dangerous.

WIFE (pouting): That does not seem like love to me. What have I done for you to mistrust me? Do the right thing and tell me!

NARRATOR: The wife hounded Bisclavret on the matter.

WIFE: If you truly loved me, you would tell me.

NARRATOR: Finally, Bisclavret could stand her protestations no longer.

BISCLAVRET: On the road beside the woods, there is an old chapel. In front of the chapel is a big, hollowed out stone. I hide my clothes there until I am ready to come home.

NARRATOR: The wife nodded and quickly withdrew her hand. Bisclavret reached for it again, but she flinched. She would not let him touch her before he had to go away again.

SCENE 2:

Later that week. At Bisclavret's home.

NARRATOR: As soon as Bisclavret left for the forest, his wife sent for a knight who she knew loved her and would do anything for her.

KNIGHT: My lady, I am always at your service. What can I do for you?

WIFE: You must help me. My husband is a werewolf!

KNIGHT: How can that be?

NARRATOR: The wife told the knight the whole story of how she had confronted her husband about what he did when he went away and what he had told her.

WIFE: I cannot stay married to such a man!

KNIGHT: What do you wish, my love? Do you want me to take you away?

WIFE: No, I want you to stay with me. But first, you must get rid of my husband by turning him into a werewolf for good.

KNIGHT: How?

NARRATOR: The wife explained to the knight that her husband needed his clothes to turn back into a man.

WIFE: So all you have to do is go get my husband's clothes, and bring them back to me. If you do that, I will be yours forever.

KNIGHT: My love for you is greater than my fear of your husband the werewolf. I will do as you ask to make you mine.

NARRATOR: The knight went out and found Bisclavret's clothes in the hollowed out rock where he had told his wife he hid them. The knight brought the clothes back to Bisclavret's wife. The man Bisclavret never returned. This saddened all but his wife, who soon married the knight.

⚜ ACT II ⚜

SCENE:

The following year. In Bisclavret's forest.

NARRATOR: One day, the king went hunting in the forest where Bisclavret the werewolf was. The hunters and dogs found Bisclavret and were about to tear him apart, when Bisclavret saw the king and ran to him.

KING: What is this?

NARRATOR: Bisclavret kissed the king's leg and foot. The king called his companions.

KING: My lords, come quickly! Look, this beast is humbling itself to me. It has the mind of a man, and it is begging me for mercy.

NARRATOR: Bisclavret grabbed the king's stirrup and held on for his life.

KING: Chase the dogs away! Make sure no one strikes this beast.

NARRATOR: The dogs were called away.

KING: Let us leave this place. I shall extend my peace to this creature. Indeed, I will hunt no more today.

NARRATOR: The king turned away, but Bisclavret followed him. He stayed close to the king all the way back to the castle. The king let Bisclavret follow him inside.

KING: I have never seen such a wondrous beast! He shall stay in the castle. He shall be well cared for and kept from harm.

NARRATOR: Bisclavret was well-loved in his new home. He was a noble and well-behaved beast. He followed the king, whom he dearly loved, everywhere. Each night, he slept among the knights near the king.

⚜ ACT III ⚜

SCENE 1:

Several months later. At the king's castle.

NARRATOR: The king was having a feast to which all the lords in the land had been invited. Among the guests was the knight who had stolen Bisclavret's clothes and married his wife. As soon as this man entered the great hall, Bisclavret attacked him.

KING (*yelling to Bisclavret*)**:** Off, beast! Off! What are you doing attacking my guest?

NARRATOR: Bisclavret ignored the king and knocked the knight to the ground. He was about to sink his teeth into the man when the king drove him off with a stick.

KING (*to the knight*): I am sorry. He has never acted this way before.

NARRATOR: The knight was pale and shaken. He looked at Bisclavret, who had to be held back by two of the king's men, with questioning eyes. Then he hurried away. Bisclavret calmed down after he was gone.

COURTIER 1: I have never seen this beast attack another man before!

COURTIER 2: He would not act that way without a reason.

COURTIER 3: Somehow or other, the knight must have mistreated him, and now the beast wants his revenge.

SCENE 2:

Not long afterward. In the countryside where Bisclavret once lived.

NARRATOR: The king, with Bisclavret by his side, went out hunting and spent the night in a country estate. Upon hearing that the king was in the area, Bisclavret's former wife went to pay him a visit. She was greeted at the door by one of the king's courtiers.

COURTIER 1: May I help you?

WIFE: I come with gifts and greetings for my king.

COURTIER 1: He is in the great hall. You may go see him.

NARRATOR: Bisclavret, who had been sleeping by the king's side, awoke as soon as his wife opened the door. When he saw the woman who had betrayed him, he lunged at her.

KING (*shouting*): Beast! Restrain yourself! Men, seize him!

NARRATOR: Several men immediately surrounded Bisclavret and were about to kill him when a wise man stopped them.

WISE MAN: Wait! (*to the king*) My lord, listen to me! This beast has never touched anyone, or shown any wickedness, except to this woman and her husband.

KING: That is true.

WISE MAN: By the faith that I owe you, he has some grudge against them both.

KING: Does that mean he has the right to attack them in this way?

WISE MAN: I know not. But this woman is the wife of the knight you used to like so much, and who has been missing for so long.

KING (*sadly*): We never could find what became of him....

WISE MAN: Why not put this woman to torture and see if she will tell you why the beast hates her?

NARRATOR: The king decided to take the wise man's advice.

SCENE 3:

The following day. In the castle's torture chamber.

NARRATOR: The wife entered the torture chamber and nearly fainted.

WIFE (*panicked*): Wait! I will tell you everything.

NARRATOR: The wife then told all about her husband and how she had betrayed him by taking all his clothes away.

KING (*shaking his head*): So this beast is the husband you betrayed?

WIFE: Yes. I am quite certain that this beast is my husband.

KING (*to his guard*)**:** Take this faithless woman away.

GUARD: Yes, my lord. (*to himself*) I will take her to her prison cell, though I would rather feed her to the beast.

NARRATOR: The guard and wife were nearly out the door when the king suddenly thought of something.

KING: Wait! Woman, where are your husband's clothes? What have you done with them?

WIFE: I hid them at home.

KING (*to his guard*)**:** Take her to show you where they are. But be sure to bring her back.

GUARD: Yes, my lord.

SCENE 4:

The next day. In the castle's great hall.

NARRATOR: The clothes were brought back and placed in front of Bisclavret in the great hall. Everyone stood and watched to see what he would do.

COURTIER 2: He has not even moved.

COURTIER 3: I did see him twitch when the clothes were placed in front of him.

KING: Why does he refuse to put them on?

WISE MAN: My lord, you are not doing it right. This beast would never put his clothes on in front of you. He is ashamed to dress here, in front of all these people.

KING: Yes. I suppose you are right.

WISE MAN: Have him led to your chamber, and bring the clothes with him.

KING (*to one of his men*)**:** Do as the wise man says. (*to all*) We will leave him alone

and see if he turns into a man.

NARRATOR: A short while later the king went into his chamber. The knight—the man we call Bisclavret—was fast asleep on the king's royal bed.

KING (*weeping for joy*)**:** It is he! My loyal knight is found.

WISE MAN (*looking at drawing of beast hanging by king's bed*)**:** Yes, though he was never truly lost.

NARRATOR: The king went to Bisclavret and hugged and kissed him. He gave him back all the lands that were once his and more. As for his wife and her second husband, the king banished them from the kingdom.

THE END

Bisclavret (The Werewolf)
Teaching Guide

Background

About the Play

Bisclavret is adapted from one of the twelve short romances and tales in the twelfth-century *Lais of Marie de France*. The story uses the folklore of lycanthropy (a person becoming a wolf by witchcraft or magic), a subject of deep fascination to Europeans in the Middle Ages, as a backdrop for a morality tale. In the story, love is found to be a socializing force, while its betrayal has the opposite effect.

About Marie de France

Marie de France is considered by many to be the first woman novelist. Very little is known about her, except what can be learned from her writings.

Marie was born in France (hence her name, *de France*), and lived during the late twelfth and early thirteenth centuries. She was probably a noblewoman: she traveled in the high circles of one of noble birth, frequenting the court of King Henry and Eleanor of Aquitane; the subjects that concerned her—morality and courtly love—were subjects that would concern someone of higher birth; and she was well educated—she knew French, English, and Latin.

Marie lived during a time of great intellectual, social, and artistic growth. She wrote for the English court, which in her day was French-speaking as a result of the Norman conquest. Her works reached the first large and sophisticated, audience in medieval Europe.

Marie's greatest work was the *Lais*, though

WORDS TO KNOW

chamber: bedroom

courtier: a person in attendance at the royal court

knight: a nobleman and soldier

she also wrote a collection of animal fables and a supernatural tale, *St. Patrick's Purgatory.* Scholars say her literary activities probably date to between 1160 and 1215.

About the Lais of Marie de France

Marie said she wrote the *Lais* for a "noble king," probably King Henry II. The tales, which Marie wrote in French verse, are likely based on Celtic tales. They deal mostly with love and sometimes with adventure. Marie probably wrote the *Lais* between 1169 and 1199, though the earliest known manuscript dates from the mid-thirteenth century.

Making Connections

Responding to the Play

Taming the beast within: Tell students that the story of Bisclavret can be seen as an allegory that explores how to tame the beast within. Ask students if they agree that there is a beast lurking within all of us. If they agree there is a beast, ask how they think we tame it. What causes it to emerge or enrages it? Ask students what tames the beast in Marie's tale (love and loyalty). What enrages it? (betrayal)

Better left unsaid…: Ask students if they think that some things—like Bisclavret's admission that he was a werewolf—are better left unsaid, or do they think that honesty is always the best policy? Ask them to support their answers with real-life examples.

Villain or victim? Ask students why they think Bisclavret's wife acted they way she did. What would they have done had they been her?

Extension Activities

Minstrels: Explain to students that in the Middle Ages, minstrels were musicians who traveled from place to place, singing and reciting poetry to music. Invite students to perform this story as minstrels. Divide the class into small groups and assign each group one part of the play. Ask each group to turn their section into verse, the story's original form. When they are done, ask students to either sing the story or recite it with musical accompaniment—such as taped harp music or any classical piece—as minstrels did hundreds of years ago. Note: Rather than change the play back into verse, you might want to have students refer to a translation of the original, such as the *Lais of Marie de France* (Dutton, 1978).

Transformation tales: Tell students that there are many stories from all over the world in which people are transformed into mythical beasts, such as werewolves, or real creatures, such as frogs. Other tales of transformation include *Beauty and the Beast* and *The Frog Prince.* Ask students if they are familiar with any such stories. Then tell students to imagine that they have to turn into an animal. Ask them to talk about what animal they would choose and why. Have them make a mask of that animal, using whatever craft materials you have available, and hold the mask in front of them while they tell the class what animal they are and why.

Women writers: Share the biographical information about Marie de France with the class. Tell students that she may have been the first woman novelist and that she was certainly among the earliest well known women writers. Invite each student to choose one woman writer to research. Then ask students to write a one-page report on the author to share with the class.

The Three Estates (Reproducible #1): Ask students to go back to this reproducible and place Bisclavret's name in its proper estate.

Robin Hood Helps a Sorrowful Knight

A Robin Hood Legend

Characters (in order of appearance):

NARRATOR

ROBIN HOOD: the legendary outlaw

LITTLE JOHN
MUCH
WILL SCARLET } members of Robin Hood's band of outlaws

SIR RICHARD: a knight

FRIAR TUCK: a member of Robin Hood's band

ABBOT: the chief monk at St. Mary's Abbey

SHERIFF: high justice of England

CELLARER: monk in charge of ale and wine at St. Mary's Abbey

PRIOR: the second in command at St. Mary's Abbey

PORTER: the monk stationed at the gate of St. Mary's Abbey

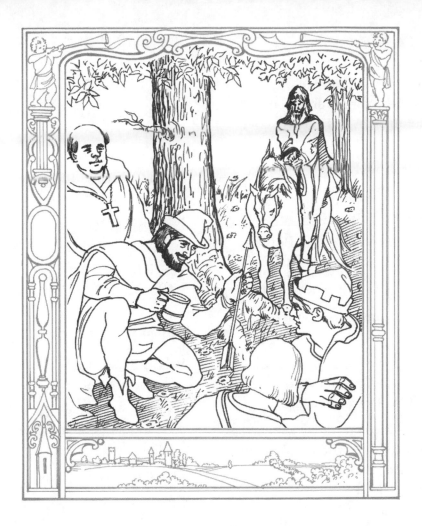

❧ ACT I ❧

SCENE 1:

Late twelfth century. Deep inside Sherwood Forest in Nottinghamshire, England.

NARRATOR: Robin Hood and his merry band of men rested in their favorite spot, beneath the greenwood tree.

ROBIN HOOD: My stomach tells me it is time to eat, but my mind says it is not.

LITTLE JOHN: Come, Master. We will have fish and venison and spiced wine.

ROBIN HOOD (*shaking his head*): No. I cannot dine until I have a strange and unknown guest to dine with us.

LITTLE JOHN (*grinning*): A wealthy guest?

ROBIN HOOD (*laughing*): Of course! A guest who can pay for the best!

LITTLE JOHN: Say no more, Master. I will go with Much and Will Scarlet to find such a guest.

ROBIN HOOD: I shall have the banquet waiting.

NARRATOR: Little John, Much, and Will Scarlet grabbed their bows and arrows and left the forest in search of a wealthy guest.

SCENE 2:

Later that day. Beside a road outside Sherwood Forest.

NARRATOR: Little John, Much, and Will Scarlet hid behind some trees to watch the road. They saw nothing but honest working people—ploughmen, swineherds, quarrymen, shepherds, and the like—

returning home from a hard day's work. They had been there for several hours. Evening was coming. It was getting cold and dark.

MUCH (*shivering*)**:** How I long for the fireside and a good warm meal.

WILL SCARLET: I add my voice to yours.

LITTLE JOHN: And I add mine. But duty is duty. Let us wait a while longer.

NARRATOR: A fine rain began to fall.

MUCH: Let us go before we are soaked through.

LITTLE JOHN (*whispering*)**:** Wait. Look there. Down the road. Someone on horseback. Perhaps it is our guest.

NARRATOR: The three outlaws watched a man ride toward them in the fading light. He wore a knight's clothes—though they were quite worn—and rode a worn-out horse. It was impossible to see the man's face: he hung his head and rested his chin on his chest.

MUCH (*softly*)**:** Is that a knight?

WILL SCARLET: If so, he is truly sorrowful.

MUCH: I know not which is sadder, his ragged clothes or his ragged horse.

LITTLE JOHN: Let us bring him back to dine with us. If appearances deceive, we will all be richer before long. If not, then this man needs a good meal and his horse a good rest.

NARRATOR: Little John stepped out from behind the tree and grabbed the knight's horse by the bridle.

SIR RICHARD (*lifting his head, startled*)**:** Who are you? What do you wish from me?

LITTLE JOHN: Welcome, sir, to the greenwood. And greetings from my master.

SIR RICHARD: Who is your master?

LITTLE JOHN: Robin Hood.

SIR RICHARD: I have heard much about Robin Hood.

LITTLE JOHN: Now you shall get to meet him. You shall dine with us tonight in Sherwood Forest.

NARRATOR: Little John began to lead Sir Richard, by his horse, into the forest.

SIR RICHARD: Wait! I am a poor guest. Poor in spirits. (*to himself*) Poor in worldly goods.

LITTLE JOHN: That is no matter.

WILL SCARLET: Besides, you and your horse are cold and wet.

MUCH: You must also be hungry. Robin Hood will generously feed both horse and rider.

SIR RICHARD: But....

LITTLE JOHN (*interrupting*)**:** The matter is settled.

NARRATOR: Sir Richard hung his head as Little John, Much, and Will Scarlet led him deeper and deeper into Sherwood Forest.

SCENE 3:
A short while later. Under the greenwood tree.

NARRATOR: Robin Hood stood to greet his men and his guest.

ROBIN HOOD: Welcome to Sherwood Forest. Come, the feast is spread. My men will take care of your horse.

SIR RICHARD (*dismounting*)**:** I am Sir Richard of the Lea. You must be Robin Hood.

ROBIN HOOD: You have heard of me?

SIR RICHARD: Yes.

ROBIN HOOD: Some call me a good fellow. Some call me a thief.

SIR RICHARD: Right now, I only know to call you Robin Hood.

ROBIN HOOD: That is true enough. Now, come dine with me.

NARRATOR: Robin Hood, Sir Richard, and Robin's men feasted on roast venison, eels boiled in oil, and roast boar. For dessert they had cheese, nuts, apples, plums, and peaches. They washed it all down with spiced wine. Sir Richard smiled at Robin Hood when he finished.

SIR RICHARD: Thank you, sir. I have not eaten so well for a long time.

ROBIN HOOD: I am glad you enjoyed it. For it is our custom here to make guests pay for their meals. Now, Sir Richard, please tell me what money you have about you.

SIR RICHARD (*blushing*)**:** I should not be ashamed, but I am. I tell you the truth, that I have but ten shillings. And that is all the money that Sir Richard of the Lea has in all the world.

ROBIN HOOD: By your leave, Little John had best have a look all the same.

NARRATOR: Robin Hood nodded at Little John, who stood to perform this familiar ritual. He checked their guest's purse, his cloak pockets, and his saddlebags. Ten shillings was all he found.

ROBIN HOOD: You are an honest knight. But how did you come to be so poor? Have you no castle, lands, or cattle?

SIR RICHARD: A year ago I had. But ill luck befell me.

ROBIN HOOD: Perhaps I can help you. Will you tell me more?

SIR RICHARD (*with a heavy sigh*)**:** I have a son. He is just twenty years old. Last year he accidentally killed man in a joust. My

son was not to blame. But the man he killed had been powerful. His kinsmen had my son thrown into prison. I paid all the money I had to ransom him, and still the sheriff said it was not enough. I needed four hundred pounds more.

ROBIN HOOD: What did you do?

SIR RICHARD: I went to St. Mary's Abbey, in York. I knew the Abbot there.

FRIAR TUCK: A man ungodly, greedy, and proud.

SIR RICHARD: Yes, but wealthy. The abbey swims in gold.

ROBIN HOOD: Did the Abbot give you the money? Is your son free?

SIR RICHARD: Yes. And Yes. But ....

ROBIN HOOD: Go on.

SIR RICHARD: The Abbot's terms were harsh. He gave me a year to repay the four hundred pounds, or he would take all I have—my castle, my lands, and my cattle.

ROBIN HOOD: And now the year is up?

SIR RICHARD (*hanging his head*)**:** Yes, but I cannot pay. When your men stopped me, I was on my way to St. Mary's to beg the Abbot for a few month's grace. But I fear I shall not win it.

FRIAR TUCK (*shaking his head*)**:** You never will. I know that Abbot well. He does not have a kind bone in his body.

WILL SCARLET: Have you no friends who will help you?

SIR RICHARD: While I was rich, I had many friends. But no more. Now I have no friends.

ROBIN HOOD: Many have found Robin Hood a friend in their troubles. (*He turns to Will Scarlet.*) Go to the strong box, Will, and fetch four hundred pounds. And find a horse and armor and suit of clothing

fit for our good friend's station. He will need them in the morning.

NARRATOR: Will went to do as he was told.

SIR RICHARD (*moved*): I can hardly speak my thanks. (*He pauses.*) Tell me, when will I pay you back?

ROBIN HOOD: Twelve months from today. Here, under my greenwood tree.

SIR RICHARD: In a year then, my friend.

FRIAR TUCK (*clapping*): To sleep now, everyone to sleep. It is late, and we must get up early to see our friend off.

LITTLE JOHN: But he cannot ride unattended! Whoever heard of a knight without a squire?

ROBIN HOOD: You are right, Little John. And the job shall be yours.

LITTLE JOHN (*grinning*): Imagine a squire six feet seven inches tall!

NARRATOR: Everyone laughed as they found their sleeping places for the night.

✥ ACT II ✥

SCENE 1:
The next morning. Under the greenwood tree.

NARRATOR: Will Scarlet brought Sir Richard the four hundred pounds, new clothes, and a strong, handsome horse.

SIR RICHARD: Thank you. I will ride this horse with joy on my long journey.

NARRATOR: Sir Richard put the money in his saddlebags. Then he wrapped the good clothes in a bundle and put them on his horse.

WILL SCARLET: Will you not wear the fine clothes?

NARRATOR: Just then, Little John and Robin Hood joined them.

SIR RICHARD: I would rather travel poorly clad.

WILL SCARLET: But why?

SIR RICHARD: I want to test the Abbot's charity before I pay my debt.

LITTLE JOHN (*slapping his thigh*): That is a wonderful idea! Let me put on some old, ragged clothes. Then we will be off.

NARRATOR: While Little John changed, Sir Richard and Robin Hood said their good-byes.

SIR RICHARD: I will forever remember your kindness.

ROBIN HOOD (*clasping Sir Richard's hand*): Go, good and gentle knight. I look forward to seeing you again in twelve month's time.

NARRATOR: Sir Richard and Little John set off on their long journey to York and St. Mary's Abbey.

SCENE 2:

Three days later. At St. Mary's Abbey.

NARRATOR: A merry feast was taking place inside the abbey.

ABBOT (*clasping his fat, dimpled hands*): Today is the day Sir Richard's lands will become mine!

SHERIFF: And what a fine estate it is!

CELLARER: Are you sure, Lord Abbot, that he will be unable to pay his debt?

ABBOT: Yes! I have secretly watched Sir Richard this past year and I know he has no money to repay me.

PRIOR (*meekly*): I think…

ABBOT (*impatient*): What is it? Speak up!

PRIOR: I think your wrong Sir Richard to seize his castle and his lands and humble him so.

ABBOT (*angry*): You fret me like a flea in my beard. Save your breath. (*He looks out the window.*) I wonder, will he keep his day?

PRIOR: He may arrive here yet. It is still an hour until noon.

SHERIFF: He will not come. But never fear. We will find a way to get his lands from him.

SCENE 3:

A short while later. At the abbey gate.

NARRATOR: Sir Richard and Little John tied their horses to an iron ring in the abbey wall. Then they knocked on the gate. The porter answered.

PORTER: Yes?

SIR RICHARD: I would like to see the Abbot.

NARRATOR: The porter looked the two ragged men up and down with distaste.

PORTER: If it is food and shelter you want…

SIR RICHARD (*interrupting*): Please tell the Abbot that Sir Richard of the Lea is here to see him.

PORTER (*surprised*): Sir Richard?

NARRATOR: The porter stood in disbelief until Little John took a step closer to him.

PORTER: Come with me.

NARRATOR: Sir Richard followed the porter into the main hall.

SCENE 4:

Moments later. Inside the main hall.

NARRATOR: Sir Richard walked directly up to where the Abbot was sitting and fell to his knees.

SIR RICHARD: Lord Abbot, I am here to keep my day.

ABBOT (*roughly*): Have you brought my money?

SIR RICHARD: Alas! I have not so much as one penny upon my body.

NARRATOR: The Abbot did not try to hide his smile.

ABBOT: Then your land, your castle, and your cattle all belong to me!

SIR RICHARD (*blushing*): My good Lord Abbot. I ask a few month's grace. I have had bad luck. My….

NARRATOR: The Abbott slammed down his silver goblet so that wine splashed all over the table.

ABBOT: Not even a half-day more!

SIR RICHARD: I ask your mercy. Please do

not strip me of my lands and reduce a true knight to poverty.

NARRATOR: Sir Richard looked around the room pleadingly. His eyes rested on the sheriff.

SIR RICHARD: You are a man of law. Won't you help me in my time of need?

SHERIFF (*nudging the Abbot*): This is no business of mine, but maybe I can help. (*to the Abbot*) Will you not ease some of his debts, Lord Abbot?

ABBOT (*sighing*): Pay me three hundred pounds, Sir Richard, and I will give you quittance of your debt.

SIR RICHARD: You know, Lord Abbot, that it is as easy for me to pay four hundred pounds as three hundred. Won't you give me more time to pay my debt?

ABBOT: No! Not another day!

SIR RICHARD: You will do no more for me?

ABBOT (*angry*): Enough! Either pay your debt or release your land and be gone from my hall.

NARRATOR: Sir Richard, who had been kneeling all this time, rose to his feet.

SIR RICHARD: Abbot, you are a false, lying priest! You and your monks befoul your habits and the holy name you bear.

ABBOT (*rising*): Get out of my hall or I will call my man!

SIR RICHARD: Do not bother. I will call my man instead.

NARRATOR: Sir Richard raised a horn to his lips and blew. Little John lumbered into the room carrying a large, leather bag, which he handed to Sir Richard. The knight turned it over and emptied a pile of gold money onto the table in front of the Abbot.

SIR RICHARD: Remember, Lord Abbot,

that you promised me quittance of my debt for three hundred pounds. I will not give you one penny more.

NARRATOR: The Abbot's head drooped and his face sagged as he watched Sir Richard count out three hundred pounds.

SIR RICHARD: Now, Lord Abbot, I have paid my dues. I will leave this place.

NARRATOR: Before they left, Little John looked long and hard at the Sheriff and the Abbot's men.

LITTLE JOHN: Now I know your faces as well as your hearts. I hope we meet again in Sherwood Forest.

NARRATOR: Fear filled the hall as Little John followed Sir Richard out of the abbey.

❧ ACT III ❧

SCENE 1:
One year later. Outside Sherwood Forest.

NARRATOR: Little John, Much, and Will Scarlet were once again looking for a guest to bring back to the greenwood. The road was quiet.

MUCH: I wonder if we shall see Sir Richard pass this way on his way into the forest.

WILL SCARLET: I hope this year has been good to him.

LITTLE JOHN: Hush! I see our guest, and it looks like he can pay us well.

NARRATOR: The men watched as a monk approached leading seven packhorses and guarded by fifty men.

LITTLE JOHN: Loosen your swords.

MUCH: We are only three. I fear we will meet disgrace.

LITTLE JOHN (*ignoring him*): Bend your bows. That monk that leads the band, I met him at St. Mary's Abbey.

NARRATOR: Little John, Much, and Will Scarlet stepped in front of the Cellarer with their bows drawn.

LITTLE JOHN: Stop, you false monk. Or we will let these arrows fly.

NARRATOR: The Cellarer stopped and quickly looked for help. But his guards, upon seeing Robin Hood's men, had fled.

LITTLE JOHN: Come. My master is waiting for you.

NARRATOR: The Cellarer was too frightened and angry to speak. He let Little John and the others lead him and his packhorses into Sherwood Forest.

SCENE 2:

A short while later. Under the greenwood tree.

NARRATOR: Little John led the monk to Robin Hood.

LITTLE JOHN: I have brought you a guest from St. Mary's Abbey.

ROBIN HOOD: Welcome! So, you are from St. Mary's? What is your office?

CELLARER: I am the cellarer. I look to the ale and the wine.

ROBIN HOOD: High Cellarer, I welcome you. Come. Eat. Drink. I think you will enjoy our wine.

NARRATOR: The monk's trembling did not prevent him from gobbling a good amount of food and washing it down with plenty of Robin Hood's best wine.

ROBIN HOOD: You have eaten well. Now, let us settle our accounts.

CELLARER (*choking on his wine*): What accounts?

ROBIN HOOD: Surely you are here to settle Sir Richard's debts.

CELLARER: I know not what you are talking about!

ROBIN HOOD: What have you, sir, in your saddlebags?

CELLARER: I've twenty marks, to see me through my journey.

ROBIN HOOD: If that is all, I shall not touch one shilling. But if you have lied, High Cellarer, your deceit shall cost you dear.

NARRATOR: Robin Hood nodded at Little John, who emptied the monk's saddlebags on the ground. They contained eight hundred pounds of silver and gold.

ROBIN HOOD (*clapping his hands*): Thank you, High Cellarer. Now go in peace. Tell your Abbot that he has paid Sir Richard's debt twice over.

CELLARER: But....

ROBIN HOOD: If you had told the truth, he need have paid it only once. Now go.

NARRATOR: The Cellarer started to speak again but thought better of it. He climbed back on his horse and, leaving all he had brought with him behind, was led back to the highway.

SCENE 3:

A short while later. Under the greenwood tree.

NARRATOR: The sun was setting when Sir Richard came to Sherwood Forest. The knight found Robin Hood and his men sitting under the greenwood tree.

SIR RICHARD: I come to pay you four

hundred pounds, the money I borrowed one year ago this very day.

ROBIN HOOD: Keep your money. You owe me nothing. It has been paid—with interest—by the High Cellarer of St. Mary's.

NARRATOR: Robin Hood then went on to tell Sir Richard of the day's first guest.

SIR RICHARD: That is a wonderful story. But are you sure you will not take my gold?

ROBIN HOOD: No. I could not take the money twice.

NARRATOR: Robin Hood looked at the wagon Sir Richard had brought with him. It was piled high with bows, bowstrings, and arrows.

ROBIN HOOD: What are these hundred bows and arrows?

SIR RICHARD: They are my humble gifts to you. One hundred bows of the finest yew with bowstrings twisted by my wife and her maids. One hundred leather quivers. And, inside each quiver, a score of shafts feathered with the plumes of peacocks.

NARRATOR: Robin Hood pulled one of the bows from the wagon and admired it.

ROBIN HOOD: I accept your gift with all my heart.

NARRATOR: Robin Hood and Sir Richard looked at each other in silence.

SIR RICHARD: I must return before my lady begins to worry.

ROBIN HOOD: If ever you need a friend, you have one in the greenwood.

SIR RICHARD: That I know. And if ever you are in need, come to me and my lady. The walls of Castle Lea shall be battered down before I will let harm befall you.

NARRATOR: Robin Hood nodded his

thanks. Then he and each of his men picked up a flaming torch to light Sir Richard's way out of the forest. At the edge of Sherwood, Sir Richard kissed Robin upon the cheeks.

SIR RICHARD: I am one who says Robin Hood is a good fellow.

NARRATOR: Robin clasped Sir Richard's hand. The knight smiled at his friends, turned onto the King's highway, and was gone.

THE END

Robin Hood Helps a Sorrowful Knight

Teaching Guide

WORDS TO KNOW

abbey: a monastery, or house for persons under religious vows, such as monks and nuns

abbot: the superior of a monastery for men

cellarer: the official in charge of provisions, i.e., food and drink

joust: a match fought with lances by two knights

kinsmen: relatives

knight: a nobleman and soldier

porter: a doorman

prior: the second in charge, after the abbot, of a monastery

squire: the shield- or armor-bearer of a knight

Background

About the Play

Robin Hood Helps a Sorrowful Knight is adapted from what scholars believe may have been the first of the many stories about the legendary English outlaw Robin Hood. The story of Robin Hood, the knight, and the Abbot of St. Mary's was first recorded in *The Gest of Robin Hood*, a long poem composed in the fifteenth century, perhaps as early as 1400. This is one of the first *written* versions of the story. Scholars believe, however, that stories about the legendary prince of thieves were first told about 200 years earlier.

About the Legend of Robin Hood

Scholars believe the legend of Robin Hood, the English outlaw who stole from the rich

and gave to the poor, began in the 1300s. The first written reference to Robin Hood is in the long poem *Piers Plowman*, written about 1377, and the oldest surviving versions of the stories—five poems or ballads and a fragment of a play, which include the *Gest*—date from the fifteenth century and later.

Who was Robin Hood? Some scholars think that the character is based on a real person, though they cannot agree on whom. Some think Robin Hood was Robert Fitz-Ooth, the Earl of Huntingdon, born 1160, while others think he was a contemporary of Edward II, who lived in the early fourteenth century. Then there is the intriguing reference to "Robertus Hood fugitivus" in Yorkshire records dated 1230. The problem is that there are no records from that time showing knowledge of Robin Hood or his deeds. It is this that causes a good many scholars to doubt that there ever was a real Robin Hood. They believe that the character is entirely fictional, although parts of the legend may be loosely based on stories about other, real, thirteenth century outlaws. In the end, it doesn't seem to matter whether or not Robin Hood was a real person. The character has survived for more than six hundred years as a hero in ballads, poems, books, plays, and movies, regardless of his authenticity.

Why has the legend lasted so long? From the beginning, the story was very popular. Three of its main elements—the sheriff, the forest, and archery—were of great interest to English people in the Middle Ages. The sheriff, along with such characters as the Abbot of St. Mary's, symbolized a major problem of the Middle Ages—the corruption of and exploitation by men who had power and wealth. Robin Hood's duping and robbing the rich and powerful made him a real hero, especially with common people. The forest was something nearly everyone knew—during the thirteenth century, nearly half of England was still covered with thick forest. And the appeal of archery was far-reaching—it was a skill shared by all social classes and, sometimes, both genders.

Because the story was so popular, it spread quickly. The earliest surviving versions of the stories begin with such phrases as, "Lithe and listin, gentilmen," indicating that the stories were recited to an audience. Thus the stories spread from family to family and village to village by word of mouth. The teller of the tales was often a minstrel, a medieval entertainer who traveled from place to place, bringing his songs and stories with him. The popular legend traveled far and wide, and fast. By the end of the fifteenth century, Robin Hood was known in a wide range of towns in northern and southern England, as well as in Scotland. When printing was invented, the stories were written down. Today, they are known all over the world.

Making Connections

Responding to the Play

Good fellow or thief? Remind students that in Act I, Scene 3, Robin Hood says to Sir Richard, "Some call me a good fellow. Some call me a thief." Ask students if, based on this play, they would call Robin Hood a good fellow or a thief? Why? Do they think it is possible to be both? Ask them to explain their answers.

Do two wrongs make a right? Invite students to discuss if they feel Robin Hood was justified in robbing the cellarer to, as he put it, pay Sir Richard's debt. Why or why not?

Appearances deceive: Ask students what they would expect an outlaw living in the forest to be like. What would they expect an abbot to be like? How do Robin Hood and

the Abbot of St. Mary's differ from their expectations? Are people always what they appear? Ask students to share examples of times when they have been deceived by a person's appearance.

A friend in need…: Review with students the scene in which Will Scarlets asks Sir Richard, "Have you no friends who will help you?" (Sir Richard replies, "When I was rich, I had many friends. But no more." Act I, Scene 3.) Discuss the meaning of friendship. Ask students if they think Sir Richard's friends were real friends. Why or why not?

Making a legend: Ask students to think about why Robin Hood, if he ever existed, has become a legend. What made him so popular that his stories would be told for more than five hundred years? Ask students if they can think of anyone today who has the potential to become a legend. If so, who, and why?

Extension Activities

Picture this: Divide students into small groups and ask each group to make a poster advertising the play *Robin Hood Helps a Sorrowful Knight.* Each group should try to create artwork and a tagline that convey the subject of the play. Display the completed posters. Ask students to look at them and think about the differences and similarities in the ways they and their classmates visually represented the play. Ask students what about each poster makes them want to see the play. Why? You may want to extend this to a discussion of advertising in general; what works to get students' attention and what does not?

Pass it along: This activity—a variation of the game "telephone"—will help students see how a story can and does change as it is passed from one person to the next. First, ask a volunteer to write a brief story about

something funny that happened to him or her. Then ask that student to read the story to another student. Ask that student to tell the story to another student, and that student to tell it to another student, and so on until everyone in the class—including you—has heard the story. Ask the final listener to write down the story. Then read both versions aloud to the class. Students will probably have a good laugh over how the stories compare. Point out that stories of Robin Hood were passed along orally for two hundred years before they were written down. Ask them to think about how the stories might have changed through the years.

Rhyme time! Ask each student to research a legendary hero from American folklore (for example, Davy Crockett, Johnny Chapman/ Appleseed, Pocahontas). Ask each student to compose a ballad (a rhyming story suitable for singing)—the form of some of the first stories about Robin Hood—about his or her hero. The ballad can be about the hero's entire life, or just about a portion of it. Invite students to share their ballads with the class.

Money matters: Ask students to calculate how much money Robin Hood "made" on his loan to Sir Richard (400 pounds). More advanced students can figure out how much interest he made (100 percent).

Further Reading

For Students:
Robin and His Merry Men: Ballads of Robin Hood (Walck 1970).

Some Merry Adventures of Robin Hood by Howard Pyle (Scribners 1954).

Robin Hood: His Life and Legend by Bernard Miles (Checkerboard 1989).

Robin Hood of Sherwood Forest by Ann McGovern (Scholastic 1991).

The Making of the Magna Carta

A Dramatization

Characters (in order of appearance):

NARRATORS 1-2

ARCHBISHOP WALTER: Archbishop of Canterbury

KING JOHN: King of England

BARON

BARON'S WIFE

PEASANTS 1-3

WARDEN: one of King John's men

PRIOR

ARCHBISHOP LANGTON: Archbishop of Canterbury, after Archbishop Walter

ROBERT FITZWALTER: a baron

BARONS 1-2

WILLIAM MARSHAL: one of King John's advisers

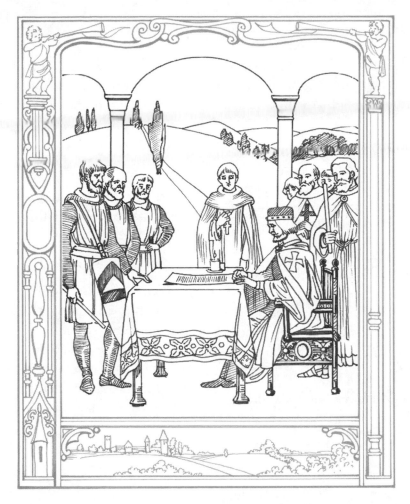

⚜ ACT I ⚜

SCENE 1:

May 27, 1199. Inside Westminster Abbey, London, England.

NARRATOR 1: After the death of his brother, King Richard, John quickly presented himself to be crowned king. The youngest son of King Henry II stood before a crowd of English nobles and churchmen and took his coronation vows.

ARCHBISHOP WALTER: Do you, John, swear to love and protect the Church of Rome.

KING JOHN: I swear it.

ARCHBISHOP WALTER: Do you swear to love and protect your people?

KING JOHN: I swear it.

ARCHBISHOP WALTER: Do you swear to see that true justice is carried out in your kingdom?

KING JOHN: I swear it.

NARRATOR 1: John made these promises with ease, but not sincerity. While he wanted the power of the throne, he did not concern himself much with its responsibilities.

SCENE 2:

Early 1204. Inside an English nobleman's castle.

NARRATOR 1: Soon after John became king, he prepared to sail for France. The French king, Philip, was trying to capture English possessions on the Continent.

NARRATOR 2: John called his barons to come fight with him. He was using the

feudal custom that said, when called upon by their overlord, men must fight or pay for professional soldiers to fight in their place.

NARRATOR 1: But many of John's barons refused to go, saying that their feudal obligations did not extend to fighting across the Channel. This angered John greatly, and he set off to fight with less of a force than he would have liked.

NARRATOR 2: John's fight was unsuccessful. By 1204, he had lost much of the land held by his ancestors. John blamed the barons who had refused to follow him into war for this defeat. And he expressed his anger toward them with greed and cruelty.

BARON: I am afraid I have bad news from Westminster, dear.

BARON'S WIFE: What is it? Has King John increased our taxes yet again?

BARON: Yes, but it is more than that. The king has demanded that I surrender our son to him as a hostage.

BARON'S WIFE (*shocked*): A hostage? But why?

BARON: To ensure my good behavior.

BARON'S WIFE: I do not understand. What have you done to offend him?

BARON: The king is taking many sons hostage. He is punishing all the barons who did not go to France with him.

BARON'S WIFE: You gave him a large sum of money to excuse you from that battle, did you not?

BARON: Yes, but he now says that was not enough. He is sure there is some sort of conspiracy against him.

BARON'S WIFE: Is there?

BARON: There are many disgruntled barons. This king's taxes are high and his fees are unreasonable. But more than that.

He persecutes as he pleases, seizing property and person without regard to the law. And now, this hostage-taking….

BARON'S WIFE (*crying out*): I will not let him have our son!

BARON: I am afraid we must. If we do not, he will take our lands and brand me an outlaw. There will be a price on my head.

NARRATOR 1: The wife put her face in her hands and wept bitterly.

NARRATOR 2: The baron's heart hardened against the king. With the constant struggle for power in the Middle Ages, the alliance between a king and his barons was seldom an easy one. King John's actions made it worse.

SCENE 3:

A summer day during King John's rule. In a rural English village.

NARRATOR 1: Like most men of the Middle Ages, King John loved to hunt. He had all of the royal forests at his disposal, for these forests were reserved for the king. Common people were strictly forbidden to hunt there.

NARRATOR 2: There were many villages within the royal forests. The villagers would often surround the fields they farmed with ditches and hedges to keep forest animals from eating their crops.

NARRATOR 1: John often showed his cruelty by putting his pleasure above his subjects' survival. This following was not an uncommon occurrence during his reign.

PEASANT 1: Look! Smoke! Over on the edge of our neighbor's wheat field!

NARRATOR 1: The peasant and his son ran toward the burning hedge. They were met on the way by several other villagers.

40

PEASANT 1: What is happening?

PEASANT 2: The king's warden and his foresters are setting fire to our hedges!

NARRATOR 1: The peasants ran to the warden and stood, dumbstruck, staring at the flames consuming their protective hedges. One of them finally spoke up.

PEASANT 3: Why have you set fire to these hedges?

WARDEN (*angry*): Who are you to question the actions of an officer of the king?

PEASANT 1 (*meekly*): Can you not at least tell us why?

WARDEN: The impudence! I should arrest you for it, were you not to be punished in another way soon enough. Now be off with you. I must finish preparing for the king's hunt.

NARRATOR 1: With that, the warden continued his destruction, and the peasants knew the reason for it. The king was coming to hunt in the nearby forest. And he wanted his game fattened—on their crops—before he came.

NARRATOR 2: The peasants took turns watching the fields and trying to drive off the forest animals that came to graze there. They saved a good deal of grain that way. But it didn't matter much in the end. During the hunt, the king and his men trampled the peasants' tall grain fields. John and his men gave nary a thought to the hunger that would be the result of their carelessness.

SCENE 4:
July, 1205. Canterbury, England.

NARRATOR 1: When John first became king, there was another powerful ruler in England. His name was Hubert Walter, and he was Archbishop of Canterbury, head of the Church of England. As the Archbishop, Walter had much power. But he had even more because John's predecessor, King Richard, had often left him in charge of the country during his long absences.

NARRATOR 2: John resented Archbishop Walter's power and was delighted to get news of the Archbishop's death in July, 1205. King John rushed to Canterbury. He couldn't wait to fill the position with someone who would do as he was told.

KING JOHN (*to the monks and prior of Canterbury*): I demand that you elect John Grey, Bishop of Norwich, as your new Archbishop.

NARRATOR 1: John's demand was met with silence.

KING JOHN: Have you ears?

PRIOR: Yes, Sire. But I am afraid we cannot do as you ask. We have already elected Reginald, one of our own.

NARRATOR 1: The king flew into a rage.

KING JOHN: How dare you? I will let the Pope know of your treachery. And I will see to it that John Grey is given this office!

NARRATOR 1: Both King John and the prior of Canterbury sent messages to the Pope, Innocent III, who settled the matter by appointing another person entirely. His choice for the job was Cardinal Stephen Langton, an Englishman teaching at the University of Paris.

NARRATOR 2: John erupted in a fury when he learned of Pope Innocent's action. He expelled the prior and monks from Canterbury and seized the church and its holdings there. He vowed that the only person he would accept for Archbishop was John Grey.

NARRATOR 1: When the Pope learned of

John's actions, he placed England under an interdict. That meant the churches were closed. There were no masses, no marriage blessings, no last rites. This hurt the common people much more than the nonreligious king.

NARRATOR 2: In fact, John saw the interdict as an excuse to seize more church property. The battle between King John and the Church continued for a number of years. It wasn't until John heard that the Pope was encouraging King Philip of France to invade England that John decided to make amends with the church. He did this by agreeing to accept Stephen Langton as Archbishop of Canterbury in 1213.

◈ ACT II ◈

SCENE 1:

August 25, 1214. At St. Paul's Church, London.

NARRATOR 1: Stephen Langton, the new Archbishop of Canterbury, had heard much about King John's rule that had troubled him while he was in France. Once he was back in England, he was determined to do something about it.

NARRATOR 2: Langton thought there should be a form of written contract between a king and his subjects. He gathered a group of nobles to discuss his ideas.

ARCHBISHOP LANGTON: It gives me hope to see so many of you. Do you know why I have called you?

ROBERT FITZWALTER: I have heard that you wish to help us settle our grievances with the king. There are many.

ARCHBISHOP LANGTON: What are they?

BARON 1: He taxes and fines us beyond reason. In the 15 years since he became king, John has taxed us more often that his father did during his entire 35-year rule!

BARON 2: It is true his greed knows no bounds. He sold my daughter to a Frenchman because he bid the highest price for her!

BARON 1 (*sadly*): Your daughter may be with a Frenchman, but at least you know she is safe. John has taken my son, along with the sons of many of us here, as hostages to ensure our good behavior. I fear what will become of them. (*quietly*) I fear what he will do if he learns of this meeting. There is no justice....

ROBERT FITZWALTER (*interrupting*): No justice save that which can be bought!

NARRATOR 1: Archbishop Langton listened to the barons express their rage and frustration with King John's rule. After a while, he spoke again.

ARCHBISHOP LANGTON: We must restore to England an orderly government under the law. Otherwise, there will be civil war.

BARON 1: I am ready to fight.

BARON 2: As am I.

NARRATOR 1: Many of the barons shouted their willingness to take up arms against the king. Archbishop Langton tried to calm them.

ARCHBISHOP LANGTON: I wish to help you, but the Church's goal is peace.

BARON: How are we to have peace under John's rule?

ARCHBISHOP LANGTON: I have found a charter of Henry I. By this charter you may, if you wish it, recall your long-lost

42

rights and your former condition.

NARRATOR 1: Archbishop Langton went on to describe, in detail, the liberties granted in King Henry's charter more than one hundred years before.

ARCHBISHOP LANGTON: The charter speaks of the king's obligations to you and to all his subjects. It also speaks of your rights, including your right to stand up for what is due you.

NARRATOR 1: The barons were quiet for some moments after Archbishop Langton described the charter.

ARCHBISHOP LANGTON: If you act together, you can bring the king to restore this charter.

NARRATOR 1: The barons began talking excitedly among themselves. Then they addressed the archbishop.

ROBERT FITZWALTER: Before you, we swear that we will stand up for these rights.

BARON 1: We will fight for them. If necessary, we will die for them.

ARCHBISHOP LANGTON: And I will support you, so long as your demands remain just.

NARRATOR 1: Over the next several months, Langton worked with the barons on a list of demands to present to King John. He tried to get them past petty demands and toward requests that would mean justice for all.

SCENE 2:

January 6, 1215. At the Temple in London.

NARRATOR 1: When the barons were finally ready to present their demands to the king, he only reluctantly agreed to hear them.

KING JOHN: What manner of address is this, from vassals, to demand an audience with your king?

ROBERT FITZWALTER: We mean no disrespect, Sire. We only ask for our lawful right that you hear us out.

KING JOHN: Lawful! I decide what is lawful!

ROBERT FITZWALTER: Yes, Sire, but....

KING JOHN (*interrupting*)**:** Need I remind you that I will use force to put down any treasonous activity.

ROBERT FITZWALTER (*boldly*)**:** Force can be met with force, Sire.

NARRATOR 1: King John pretended he didn't hear FitzWalter's remark.

KING JOHN: Well then. What is it you want?

ROBERT FITZWALTER: We want you to confirm the good laws of Edward the Confessor, reissue the charter of liberties granted by Henry I, and restore all our ancient liberties.

NARRATOR 1: John reddened as he tried to control his rage against these men and their demands. Control it he must, though, for he knew that losing his temper could lead to a revolt.

KING JOHN: Your demands are a matter of importance and difficulty. I must have time to study and review them.

ROBERT FITZWALTER: We have already waited many years for these liberties. How much longer must we wait?

KING JOHN: I will give you my answer the Monday after Easter. I need that time to determine how to satisfy your grievances as well as the dignity of my crown.

NARRATOR 1: The barons reluctantly agreed to wait.

NARRATOR 2: King John did not turn his attention to the barons' demands, however. Instead, he prepared for civil war. He spent the time the barons gave him putting all of his castles in a state of defense.

SCENE 3:
April, 1215. At Stamford.

NARRATOR 1: Easter came and went, and the barons still had no word from the king. So they and their men-at-arms began assembling at Stamford.

NARRATOR 2: When John learned of the barons' activities, he sent William Marshal, one of his closest advisers, and Archbishop Langton to Stamford. He was hoping to avert civil war once more.

ARCHBISHOP LANGTON (*addressing the barons*)**:** It is the king's desire that your grievances be settled peaceably.

ROBERT FITZWALTER: We, too, desire a peaceable settlement.

WILLIAM MARSHAL: Have you a list of the exact reforms you want granted?

NARRATOR 1: The rebels handed Marshal a list. It asked that the old laws and customs be restored.

WILLIAM MARSHAL: This is it?

ROBERT FITZWALTER: Yes. And we trust that the king will immediately put his agreement to these demands in writing and affix his seal to it.

WILLIAM MARSHAL: And if he does not?

ROBERT FITZWALTER: Then we shall have no choice but to seize his castles, lands, and goods.

NARRATOR 1: Langton and Marshal brought the list of demands back to the king. John exploded after Langton and Marshall read him the long list of demands.

KING JOHN (*furious*)**:** Why, amongst these unjust demands, did not the barons ask for my kingdom also?

NARRATOR 1: King John refused the barons' ultimatum, and the civil war began.

NARRATOR 2: The rebels launched their opening attack on the royal castle at Northampton. They quickly learned that John was a tough opponent and were driven back in fifteen days.

NARRATOR 1: King John did not have long to gloat over this easy victory. Within weeks of their defeat, the rebels went on and took London. Because the rich citizens of the city had also suffered under John's harsh rule and were ripe for rebellion, the city fell easily.

NARRATOR 2: The loss of London led John to conclude that he must reach an agreement with the rebels. He asked Archbishop Langton to set up a conference with the rebel leaders and arrange for a truce until then. The meeting was set for June 15, on a little meadow on the bank of the Thames River called Runnymeade.

ACT III

SCENE:
June 15, 1215. Runnymeade.

NARRATOR 1: With each side's army visible in the distance, the king and his men met with the rebels on the appointed date.

NARRATOR 2: As Robert FitzWalter approached his king, all watched to see if he would kneel. He did not. He simply handed John a piece of parchment.

ROBERT FITZWALTER: Here, Sire, are the demands which you have indicated you are willing to grant us.

NARRATOR 1: King John dared not show his humiliation over his subject's refusal to kneel before him. He held his head high as he accepted the piece of parchment.

KING JOHN: It is true that, for the sake of peace and for the good of my kingdom, I am willing to grant certain laws and liberties. But I would never grant you such liberties as would make me your slave. Therefore, these matters must be considered by my advisers who are here with me today.

NARRATOR 1: With that, John turned and went into the tent that was set up for deliberations. Leaders from both sides followed him inside.

NARRATOR 2: Each demand was read and discussed. After many objections, King John finally agreed to nearly all of the barons' demands.

NARRATOR 1: The Articles of the Barons, as they were first called, were agreed upon and sealed by the king on June 15. Clerks spent the next three days fine-tuning the Great Charter, or, in the Latin in which the document was written, the Magna Carta.

NARRATOR 2: On June 19, 1215, the Magna Carta was complete. Archbishop Stephen Langton asked King John to place his hand on the Bible.

ARCHBISHOP LANGTON: Do you, John, King of England, swear that the conditions of this charter shall be kept in good faith and without evil intent?

KING JOHN: I swear it.

NARRATOR 1: Archbishop Langton then administered a similar oath to the barons. When they were finished, they knelt before King John and once again swore

their loyalty to him. The charter, which granted liberties "to all the free men of the kingdom," was copied and sent to every cathedral and major city in the country.

NARRATOR 2: As with other oaths he had made, however, King John had no intention of keeping this one. Nine weeks after he placed his seal on the Magna Carta, he convinced Pope Innocent to declare the charter null and void. The Pope did so on the grounds that the barons had violated the fundamental principle of feudal loyalty to an overlord.

NARRATOR 1: Civil war broke out again. The French, taking advantage of the weakness caused by the civil war, tried to invade England. When King John died the following year, in 1216, the war was still undecided. King John's former advisers, including William Marshal, knew that they had to unite the country against the foreign enemy. They reissued the Magna Carta in the name of the new king, John's nine-year-old son, Henry.

NARRATOR 2: The charter was confirmed and reissued throughout England's history. Eventually, the Magna Carta became part of the fundamental law of England. It has also become part of the basic law of democratic countries around the world.

THE END

The Making of the Magna Carta
Teaching Guide

Background

About the Play

This play is a dramatization of the events leading up to the creation of the Magna Carta, the document that was to become the foundation of the British Constitution (not a written document, simply all the principles that underlie British law) and the law of many democratic nations, including the United States. Most of the events in the play actually took place, although there is little or no record

WORDS TO KNOW

archbishop: the religious head of a province, ranking after the pope and the cardinals

baron: a nobleman; generally the tenant-in-chief of a property

charter: a written contract

feudal: relating to feudalism, the system of political organization prevailing in Europe from about the ninth to the fifteenth centuries, which is based on the relationship between a lord and a vassal.

interdict: a church judgment of condemnation that forbids most sacraments and Christian burial from an area

overlord: a supreme ruler

peasant: a member of the class of persons that works the land

prior: the second in charge, after the abbot, at a monastery

vassal: a person under the protection of a feudal lord to whom he has vowed homage and loyalty

warden: the guard of the royal forests

READ ALOUD PLAYS: THE MAKING OF THE MAGNA CARTA
Scholastic Professional Books, 1998

of conversations that occurred.

About the Magna Carta

In form, the Magna Carta was much like other medieval charters. It was handwritten in Latin on parchment and authenticated by the king's seal. (Royal charters were not signed but sealed.) It was different in that most previous charters had granted rights to special groups of people, but this one granted rights "to all the free men of the kingdom." The Magna Carta asserted the principle of the Rule of Law: All men are bound by law; no man—king, baron, or peasant—is above the law.

The Magna Carta came about primarily because many people in the late twelfth and early thirteenth centuries felt that King John had stretched his liberties too far and had infringed on the liberties of the clergy, the nobles, even the peasants. John's treatment of the nobles—persecution of his enemies, seizures of properties, taking sons as hostages to ensure fathers' obedience, and heavy taxes and fines—made them ripe for rebellion. Under the guidance of Stephen Langton, Archbishop of Canterbury, their rebellious spirit was channeled and used to meet Langton's visionary goal of a written contract between the king and his subjects that explicitly stated the rights and obligations of all. Langton's goal was achieved with the sealing of the Magna Carta on June 15, 1215.

At King John's request, Pope Innocent canceled the Magna Carta before summer's end. The charter was later upheld by John's son, Henry III, and later English kings. It eventually came to be recognized as part of the fundamental law of England. Several of its principles regarding legal and political rights were carried to other countries. The Magna Carta strongly influenced the framework of the United States Constitution.

There were 63 articles in the Magna Carta of 1215. While many of these quickly became obsolete, others have formed the basis for laws that we have with us to this day. These include an article that says the king will not sell, deny, or delay justice; another that says that no free man shall be imprisoned, deprived of property, exiled, or destroyed, except by the lawful judgment of his peers or by the law of the land.

Of the many copies of the Magna Carta that were sent throughout England in 1215, only four survive today. Two of the originals are in the British Library in London, one is in Salisbury Cathedral, and one is in Lincoln Cathedral.

Making Connections

Responding to the Play

Rule of law versus rule of man: Compare and discuss the terms "rule of law" and "rule of man." Explain that rule of law, a concept upheld in the Magna Carta, means that the government is based on laws, and all persons—kings, presidents, and common people—must obey those laws. The rule of man implies that government—whether it's run by one person or many—is above the law. Ask students find examples in the play of ways in which King John thought that he was above the law. What were some of the consequences of his behavior? Ask students: Is the United States government based on rule of law or rule of man? What are some things that King John did that the president of the United States couldn't do?

Do rights and responsibilities go together?
Tell students the saying, "To whom much is given, much is expected." Ask them what they think it means. Do they agree with it? How does it apply to King John? Did he welcome his responsibilities to his subjects as much as he welcomed his power over them? Ask students what the expression means in their lives. If they have a lot of anything—talent,

intelligence, money—should they be expected to give more in return than someone who does not have as much? Why or why not?

Old laws in modern times: Discuss how some old laws have become outdated while others remain valid in modern times. Ask students to brainstorm rules and laws that they follow today that would have been valid during the Middle Ages (i.e., you do not take what does not belong to you). Then ask them to think of rules and laws that would have meant nothing to people hundreds of years ago (i.e., stop at red lights).

Extension Activities

The Magna Carta and the U.S. Constitution: Write the following provision from the Magna Carta on the board so that students can read it: "No freeman shall be taken or imprisoned or disseised of an freehold or liberties or customs or outlawed or banished, or in any way destroyed, nor will we go [march] against him, …except by the lawful judgment of his peers, or by the law of the land." Ask students to research and find which of the first ten Amendments to the United States Constitution is derived from this provision (the Fifth Amendment) and to copy it onto a piece of paper. As a class, discuss ways in which the Fifth Amendment protects U.S. citizens.

Chart it out: If you haven't already done so, this might be a good time to draw up a set of classroom rules, or a class charter. Work together to come up with a list of rights and responsibilities for all class members. Ask several students to take notes during discussions, and one student to write the final draft.

Latin roots: Ask students if they know what *Magna Carta* means. Tell them it means "Great Charter" in Latin, the language in which the document was written. Explain that, until modern times, Latin was the dominant language of school, church, and state in Western Europe. Tell students that, although we rarely use Latin today, the language is still with us in that many of our words have Latin roots. Ask each student to brainstorm a list of ten or twenty words and then look up their roots. How many words have Latin roots? You might want to ask one or two students to tally the class total and calculate the fraction or percentage of words with Latin roots.

Sealed with a…: Explain to students that charters in the Middle Ages were not signed but sealed. Ask each student to design a seal that they think would be appropriate for their letters. For inspiration, you might share with students examples of different seals and coat of arms from Kings and Queens. As they design their seals, remind them that a seal will print backwards—for example, a "b" will print "d"—so they should take this into account in their designs. If you have older students, you might let them carve their seals out of a potato that has been cut in half. Students can then try out their seals on a soft substance such as modeling clay or use a stamp pad and paper.

The Three Estates (Reproducible #1): Ask students to go back to this reproducible (page 17) and place the names of these characters in their proper estates.

Further Reading

For Students:
Magna Carta by William F. Swindler (Grosset & Dunlap 1968).

Magna Carta by C. Walter Hodges (Coward-McCann 1966).

Medieval People by Sarah Howard (Millbrook 1992).

First Facts About the Middle Ages by Fiona MacDonald (Peter Bedrick Books 1997).

The Middle Ages (*Cambridge Introduction to World History* series) by Trevor Cairns (Cambridge University Press 1972).

The Divided Horse Blanket

A Medieval Folktale

Characters (in order of appearance):

NARRATOR

HENRY: an old peasant

GEOFFREY: Henry's friend

GILBERT REEVE: the reeve, or village overseer

JOHN: Henry's son

AGNES: John's wife

THOMAS: John's and Agnes's son

⚘ ACT I ⚘

SCENE 1:

Late summer, 1300 A.D. In the fields of a small English village.

NARRATOR: It was late morning the second day of Lord Elton's harvest. The peasants, who had been required to harvest the lord's fields before harvesting their own, were sitting in the fields enjoying the traditional dinner feast supplied by the lord of the manor.

HENRY: I have never seen a man eat as you do, my friend.

GEOFFREY (*with a mouthful of food*): I eat when there is food.

HENRY: Lord Elton has provided much food for us this day.

NARRATOR: Geoffrey nodded as he continued to eat. Then he pointed to Henry's untouched loaf of bread.

GEOFFREY: You, too, should eat while there is food in front of you.

HENRY: I shall, though first I must rest a bit.

GEOFFREY: Are you ill?

HENRY: No. I am simply tired—tired and old.

NARRATOR: Henry sighed and tore off a chunk of bread.

HENRY: I only hope I have strength to thresh my own fields after I have fulfilled my labor services to Lord Elton.

NARRATOR: Geoffrey washed his bread and cheese down with a long drink of ale. Then he shook his head with disapproval.

GEOFFREY: Old men should not be required to labor for the lord.

READ ALOUD PLAYS: THE DIVIDED HORSE BLANKET
Scholastic Professional Books, 1998

HENRY: But I am an unfree tenant, a villein, and all villeins owe the lord week-work.

NARRATOR: Geoffrey thought as he took another long drink of his ale.

GEOFFREY: You have a son. Have you thought to give him your holding in exchange for his promise to maintain you? Then the obligations to the lord—work service, rent, and fees—would be his. He would also get the land, which would allow him to marry.

HENRY: I have thought of that. But a man wants to be master of his own cottage, however humble.

NARRATOR: The reeve began shouting in the fields.

GILBERT REEVE: Back to work, all of you! This is not a holy day, but a harvest day!

NARRATOR: Geoffrey quickly stood and stuffed as much food as he could up his sleeve. Henry was still sitting when the reeve reached them.

GILBERT REEVE: Lord Elton wants this field harvested by sundown. (*He looks at Henry.*) Can you do the work, old man, or will you hire someone to do it for you?

HENRY (*indignant*): I can do it!

GILBERT REEVE: Try to move a little faster than you did this morning, then.

NARRATOR: After the reeve continued on his way, Henry struggled to his feet. Geoffrey put his hand on his friend's shoulder.

GEOFFREY: Consider what we talked about.

HENRY: I will.

SCENE 2:
That evening. In Henry's cottage.

NARRATOR: Henry and his son, John, sat on benches at the trestle table in their small cottage and ate their supper of dark bread, turnips, and ale. The hall was quiet save for the crackle of the fire, for they lived alone. Henry's wife had died giving birth to John, their only surviving child.

HENRY: You have been a good son, John. You have the gentle nature of your mother. You work hard, you do not complain.

JOHN (*softly*): What do I have to complain of? My life is like most others.

HENRY: Do you not want to marry?

JOHN: I cannot marry without land, and I will not have land until....

NARRATOR: John was afraid to finish his sentence, so Henry finished it for him.

HENRY: Until I die? You can say it. Is that not how I got this land, upon my own father's death?

NARRATOR: John nodded.

HENRY: Perhaps you will not have to wait for that day.

JOHN: What do you mean, Father?

HENRY: I have decided to transfer my holding to you now, while I live. The land will be yours, as will the obligations of work service, rents, and fees.

NARRATOR: John did not know what to say.

HENRY: In exchange, you must promise to maintain me here as a free boarder for as long as I live.

JOHN: Certainly I will take care of you, Father. Everything will be as it is now. You will keep your room, I will continue to sleep in the loft. And when you have arranged my marriage, my new wife will sleep in the loft with me.

HENRY: Good then, it is settled. After we harvest our own fields, I will go to the manor to make the transfer official. Then we will find you a good, hard-working wife.

SCENE 3:

The following week. Outside the walls of the manor.

NARRATOR: Henry went to the manor and transferred his property to John. On his way out of the walled grounds, he saw Geoffrey, coming to grind his wheat.

HENRY *(calling out)***:** My friend! Thank you for your good advice. I have just been to the manor to transfer my holdings to John.

GEOFFREY: I am glad for you. You will not have to work so hard. And John? He agrees to keep you?

HENRY: Of course. He is a good son.

GEOFFREY: Have you a written contract giving the terms of your agreement?

HENRY: No. None of us can read or write, and I will not pay one more fee to Lord Elton to have one written for me. Besides, I have John's word. I know he would never harm me.

GEOFFREY: What about when he marries? What if his wife is not so good as he?

HENRY: Have you not heard? Agnes Est will be his wife, her parents have agreed to it.

GEOFFREY: They must all be glad, especially she. With two older brothers to fight over a small plot, she stood little chance of marrying.

HENRY: That is in part why I chose her. She appears very grateful, which is a trait I want in a daughter-in-law who is to help provide my keep.

GEOFFREY: May she be as grateful after the marriage ceremony as before.

HENRY: She will be. And I will expect to see you at the ceremony.

GEOFFREY: Do you promise food and ale?

HENRY *(laughing)***:** You will have your fill, my friend.

GEOFFREY: Then I will be there.

NARRATOR: John and Agnes were married several weeks later. After a feast in the village tavern, Henry, John, and Agnes returned to their cottage. John took Agnes up to his loft and left the one room beside the hall to his father, as he had promised. At first, Agnes did act grateful. But it turned out to be only an act.

❧ ACT II ❧

SCENE:

One night several months later. Inside Henry's cottage.

NARRATOR: In no time, Agnes had claimed the cottage as her own. She treated Henry more and more like an unwelcome guest. When she saw that John was too meek to stand up to her, she got bolder and bolder. Henry was in his room one night, when he heard this argument between Agnes and John.

AGNES: You must ask your father to quit that room. He is but one person, we are two.

NARRATOR: There was a long silence. Henry wanted not to listen to the words that followed, but he could not help it.

AGNES: Well, man. Are you deaf and dumb? Do as I say.

JOHN *(meekly)***:** I cannot. I promised my father that room when he transferred the holding to me.

AGNES *(angry)***:** You were wrong to do so! You must go and tell him that, as the master of this cottage, that room is rightfully yours.

52

NARRATOR: Henry held his breath during the long silence before his son's reply.

JOHN: Where would he sleep then?

AGNES: He can have the flea-ridden loft.

JOHN: He is an old man. He will not be able to climb the ladder to reach it.

AGNES: Then let him sleep in the corner of the hall.

JOHN (*sighing*): But he is my father.

AGNES (*loudly*): And I am your wife!

NARRATOR: Again there was a long silence. But this one was followed by footsteps. Henry turned his face away from his son when the younger man entered his room.

JOHN: Father?

NARRATOR: Henry refused to answer.

JOHN: Father, please look at me. I know you must have heard the words that were just spoken. I am sorry, Father. There is nothing I can do. Agnes wants this room.

NARRATOR: Henry still did not answer. He dared not move, not even to brush away the tear that fell from his eye. John returned to the hall, where Agnes awaited him.

AGNES: Well? Did you do as you should have?

JOHN (*to himself*): I think not.

AGNES: I cannot hear you!

JOHN (*louder*): I did as you wanted.

AGNES (*smirking*): Then we will sleep in our room this night.

JOHN: No, we will sleep in it on the morrow. Let my father have it this last night.

AGNES (*angry*): Then I shall go to the loft now, alone. You can sleep in the hall.

NARRATOR: With that, Agnes climbed up to the loft and John lay down on the cold, packed dirt by the fire and tried to sleep.

❧ ACT III ❧

SCENE 1:

Nine years later, during the fall harvest. Inside Henry's cottage.

NARRATOR: Just after sunrise, John went out to the village well to fetch water. While he was gone, Agnes began shaking Henry violently, trying to wake him. Her eight-year-old son, Thomas, sat by the fire and watched her.

AGNES (*shouting*): Get up, lazy old man!

NARRATOR: Henry struggled to sit up, coughing all the while.

AGNES: You will not sleep while we do all the work in the fields. Get up and get out.

NARRATOR: John walked back into the cottage while Agnes was shouting at Henry. He winced to see how his wife treated his father. He felt powerless to stop her, yet he tried.

JOHN (*pleading*): Let him be, Agnes. He is old and sick. Can you not let him be?

AGNES: I will grant that he is old. But sick? He coughs so as to avoid work and stay by the fire all day and torment me.

JOHN: Agnes, he truly is sick. He coughs up blood. Surely you have noticed.

AGNES: He is coughing up ale for all I know. Now get him out of here. He will not lie around all day while all of us, even your young son, work to bring in the harvest.

NARRATOR: Henry, John, and Thomas stared at Agnes. Henry was too sick to care what happened to him. John was too afraid to argue with Agnes. Thomas just watched how his parents treated each other and his grandfather.

AGNES: What are you waiting for? Get out, all of you, we have fields to harvest.

NARRATOR: John went and helped his father get up.

JOHN (*softly*): Come, Father. The fresh air will do you good.

NARRATOR: Agnes went and stuck her face in John's.

AGNES: He is not to be lying around in the field, either. He will glean with Thomas while you and I cut and bind the wheat.

JOHN: Yes, Agnes.

NARRATOR: The family headed out to their fields.

SCENE 2:
A short while later. Out in the fields.

NARRATOR: John cut the tall stalks of wheat and Agnes followed behind him, binding them. Henry and Thomas followed a ways behind her, gathering any wheat that she missed. The young boy moved quickly and Henry could not keep up.

THOMAS: You are too slow, Grandfather!

HENRY (*coughing*): I was once like you, young and agile. But now I am old and sick.

THOMAS: And useless, my mother says. I hope I am never like you.

NARRATOR: Henry looked at this boy, his grandson, and feared that he had his mother's cold heart. Pain and sadness tore at him. He sat down to rest.

THOMAS: You had better hope Mother does not see you resting.

NARRATOR: Henry dismissed the young boy with a wave of his hand.

THOMAS: I am going to tell her you are not doing your share.

NARRATOR: Thomas ran ahead. Henry struggled to his feet to continue gleaning. His friend Geoffrey saw him from his field and came over to speak with him.

GEOFFREY (*hugging Henry*): My friend! You are but skin and bones. Does your family not feed you?

NARRATOR: The question was meant as a joke, but Geoffrey could tell from the look on Henry's face that he had struck close to the truth.

GEOFFREY: Is it as bad as that then?

NARRATOR: Henry looked away and started coughing. Geoffrey saw the blood Henry's coughs brought up.

GEOFFREY: You are ill. You should not be working.

NARRATOR: Henry kept his eyes averted, his shame at how his family treated him was so great.

GEOFFREY: I am sorry for you, my friend. Is there anything I can do for you?

NARRATOR: Henry shook his head and walked away. He continued to pick up bits and pieces of wheat until he reached John, Agnes, and Thomas, who were finishing their dinner in the field. Agnes stood when he reached them.

AGNES (*to Henry*): All your resting and talking caused you to miss dinner. (*to John and Thomas*) Back to work! I want this entire field harvested today.

SCENE 3:
That night. Inside the cottage.

NARRATOR: Henry slept fitfully while Agnes and John argued in their room. The old man heard their words as if they were part of a bad dream.

AGNES: You saw how poor the harvest was. He must go.

JOHN: It is not so bad as that. We have survived leaner years.

AGNES: Barely! And now we have a growing boy to feed and another on the way. Will you let our young son and this baby who is coming starve so that an old man might live?

JOHN: I cannot turn my father out.

AGNES: So you choose your father over your children?

JOHN (*pleading*): Please do not ask me to turn my father out. He would surely die.

AGNES: He is going to die anyway. Better sooner than later, so that we do not waste any of the little grain we have on him.

NARRATOR: There was a long silence.

AGNES: Think of your son. Think of this unborn child.

JOHN (*to himself*): May God forgive me. (*to Agnes*) I will do as you wish.

SCENE 4:

Early the next morning. Inside the cottage.

NARRATOR: John climbed up to the loft and woke Thomas.

JOHN: I need your help today.

THOMAS: Are you going to the fields already?

JOHN: Yes, but that is not what I want you for. I need you to do something here.

THOMAS: What is it?

NARRATOR: John turned from his son. He looked down to the hall below where his father lay sleeping. Then he looked back at his son.

JOHN: I want you to stay with your grandfather....

THOMAS: Must I watch him all day?

JOHN (*shaking his head*): No. When he wakes you are to see that he eats his fill. Then I want you to....

NARRATOR: John's throat seemed to close on his words. His eyes filled and he turned as if to leave. But then he heard his wife's heavy footsteps down below and forced himself to continue speaking.

JOHN: I want you to take your grandfather away. Perhaps to Geoffrey Richardson's cottage, by the river. Geoffrey is an old friend.

NARRATOR: Thomas looked at his father with a mixture of pity and contempt.

THOMAS: I will do as you ask.

NARRATOR: John nodded then climbed down from the loft. He went to cover his father with the blanket that had fallen off of him but stopped when his wife yelled.

AGNES: Come now! You have wasted enough time this morning.

NARRATOR: John hurried out the cottage door after his wife. A short while later, Thomas climbed down from the loft to wake his grandfather.

THOMAS: Wake up, old man!

HENRY (*to himself*): I had the most awful dream.

THOMAS: Come, Grandfather, eat. I have work to do.

HENRY: What is the hurry?

THOMAS: You must go away.

HENRY: Away? Where?

THOMAS: It does not matter. Wherever someone will have you.

NARRATOR: A look of recognition came over Henry's face.

HENRY (*sadly*)**:** Ah. Then it was not a dream.

THOMAS: Will you eat, old man?

NARRATOR: Henry shook his head.

THOMAS: Come then. Father said you might go to Geoffrey Richardson's cottage.

NARRATOR: Henry did not answer.

THOMAS: Go then. I must help my mother and father in the fields.

NARRATOR: Henry struggled to his feet.

HENRY: I am going.

THOMAS: If they ask, where shall I say you have gone?

NARRATOR: Henry did not answer. He threw his old horse blanket over his shoulders and walked out the door. Thomas followed.

THOMAS: Grandfather, wait!

NARRATOR: Henry stopped, but he did not turn around. Thomas hurried up to him and lifted the horse blanket off of his shoulders.

HENRY (*bitterly*)**:** Will you not even give me this old horse blanket?

THOMAS: Hush. You will get half.

NARRATOR: Then Thomas neatly tore the blanket in two. He gave one half to his grandfather, who silently continued on his way.

SCENE 5:

A short while later. In the fields.

NARRATOR: Thomas was still carrying the half a horse blanket when he reached the fields. When his father saw him coming, he looked away. His mother ran to him.

AGNES: Did you do it?

THOMAS: I did.

NARRATOR: Agnes smiled. Then she noticed the horse blanket John was carrying.

AGNES: Good child! You even saved the old horse blanket.

NARRATOR: John looked at his son.

JOHN: You sent him off without even a blanket?

THOMAS: I gave him half a blanket.

JOHN (*questioningly*)**:** Half?

THOMAS: I am saving the other half for you, when you are an old man.

NARRATOR: John put down his sickle and shook his fists in anger. His wife and son stepped back, for they had never seen him like this.

JOHN: Where did you take your grandfather?

THOMAS: I took him nowhere. He went alone.

JOHN (*defiantly*)**:** I am going to find him and bring him back, to *his* home.

NARRATOR: John searched everywhere, but never did find his father. The only trace of Henry was his half of the horse blanket, which John found floating in the river.

THE END

The Divided Horse Blanket

Teaching Guide

Background

About the Play

*T*he *Divided Horse Blanket* is based on one of the many versions of the classic Middle Ages story of the same name. The story was meant to warn parents about what might happen to them if they handed their land over to their children without safeguards such as a written contract. Many peasants seemed to take the story's warning to heart and transferred holdings to their children with very specific written contracts that were entered into the manorial court rolls.

About Peasants in the Middle Ages

The majority of people in the Middle Ages were peasants. This group had few rights and many obligations, primarily to their lord, who might be a member of the nobility or the clergy. Two things that determined a peasant's status were whether or not he was free and the amount of land he held, with the latter carrying the most weight. Villeins—peasants who were unfree—owed the lord substantial labor services, rents, and fees, based on the amount of land they held from him. But even

WORDS TO KNOW

boarder: a person who is provided with regular meals and lodging

glean: to gather grain or other produce left by the reapers during harvest

manor: the lord's estate

peasant: a member of the class of persons that works the land

reeve: the village overseer; the person in charge of seeing that villagers perform their duties for the lord

villein: an unfree peasant

though a peasant may not be free, if he held a fair amount of land, he was better off than a free cotter—a peasant who owned little or no land and relied on day work to eke out a living. Regardless of their status, however, most peasants' lives were very much alike. Free or unfree, landed or not, most peasants spent their days toiling in the fields for their lords and for themselves.

The peasants survived on food and drink made from the grain they cultivated in the fields. They ate little meat or fish, since all the game on the manor belonged to the lord. Winter and early spring, when the previous year's grain supplies began to run low, were lean times for peasants. Peasants also had to face intermittent crop failures, which made a hungry world even hungrier.

Most peasants lived in insubstantial thatched-roof houses or cottages of timber-frame and wattle-daub construction (the spaces between the framing were filled with oak or willow wands covered with mud and straw). The number of rooms in the house varied from one to several, depending on the peasant's wealth. The hall was the main living quarters of the house. It had an open hearth in its center where a wood or peat fire burned all day, keeping water, milk, and porridge simmering. The room was usually thick with smoke, as the only ventilation was provided by a hole in the roof, a few shuttered windows, and open doors. The floor of packed-dirt was usually covered with straw or rushes. If there was another room, it might be the master's and mistress's bedroom. There might also be a loft where children slept. There was little furniture. A typical village home had a trestle table that was disassembled at night, a couple of benches and stools, a chest for storage, straw mattresses, and perhaps a bed.

Peasant marriages, like those of the nobility, were always arranged. A man often did not marry until his father died or until his father turned his land over to him. A woman was expected to bring a dowry of money and/or other goods. Most marriages took place when the couple was in their twenties. Families were generally small due to necessity and circumstances: necessity because a family holding could feed only a limited number of people, circumstances because infant mortality was high and many adults died young.

Life expectancy in the Middle Ages was about thirty-three years of age. This does not mean that there were no old people, however, as the life expectancy was brought down by high infant mortality. While peasants generally had only a vague idea of their age (they never recorded their births and seldom had reason to tell their ages), research shows that about ten percent of the population in certain English villages was over fifty years old, the age which scribes at the time began to call a person *senex*, or old. Caring for the aged was often a problem, as the elderly generally consumed more than they produced. Many old people made written maintenance agreements with their children to guarantee their basic needs in retirement. These agreements were not always made legal, and sometimes the parent suffered as a result of them, as in *The Divided Horse Blanket*.

Making Connections

Responding to the Play

Sealed with a ...: Ask students when they think an agreement can be sealed with a handshake and when they think it should be made legally binding. Discuss Henry's reasons for not making his agreement with his son legally binding. What do students think they would have done in his shoes? Remind students that this story was told as a warning to parents not to count on the continued support of their children. Ask students if they can imagine children treating their parents like that.

58

Like father, like son: Ask students what they think prompted Thomas to tear the horse blanket in two and tell his father he was saving one half for when he was an old man. Discuss how actions speak louder than words.

The last straw: Review the end of the story with students and ask them what they think finally made John stand up to his wife, Agnes. What do they think life in John's cottage was like after he found his father's half a blanket floating in the river? What can be learned from John's behavior in the story? Invite students to look at the decisions John made during the play and discuss what he could have done differently.

The working class: An eleventh-century bishop of Laon said of peasants, "Not one free man could live without them." Ask students what they think he meant by this statement. Ask student what contributions peasants made to the economy and if they think the peasants were fairly compensated.

Matchmaker: Discuss arranged marriages with students. Do they think they are a good idea? Why or why not? Ask students to think about what they would look for in a husband or wife if they were a parent arranging their child's marriage. Ask them how this would differ from what the son or daughter might be looking for in a potential mate.

Extension Activities

Say it with pictures: Remind students that most people during the Middle Ages could neither read nor write. As a result, stories had to be told in other ways. One way was with pictures. Stories might be painted onto church walls, poured into stained glass windows, or woven into tapestries. Ask students to use pictures to tell the story of *The Divided Horse Blanket.* Read through the play a second time with the class to determine what scenes need to be illustrated. Then divide the class into that number of groups. Have each group work together to illustrate their scene. When everyone is done, hang the illustrations in a place where other students in the school can see and enjoy the story.

Practice what you preach: Have students brainstorm types of behavior adults in their lives try to teach them. Ask each student to choose one type of behavior from the list. Pass out sheets of drawing paper and have each student draw a horizontal line across the middle of the paper. Ask students to draw an example of how adults positively reinforce the behavior on one half of the paper, and negatively reinforce the behavior on the other half. For example, parents tell children not to smoke. They reinforce this positively by not smoking or by quitting smoking; they reinforce it negatively by smoking. You might want to use this activity as a springboard to discussions on how role models positively and negatively influence our lives, and how children can be positive role models for others.

Maintenance contract: As an exercise in helping students think about the give-and-take of the world, students might enjoy making their own maintenance contracts. Ask students to make a list of their needs—affection, food, shelter, clothing, transportation, entertainment. Then ask them to write down what they can and do give in return for having these needs met. Finally, ask them to combine these lists in a maintenance contract between them and their parents. Ask students if this is an agreement that they think they need to make legally binding. Why or why not?

The Three Estates (Reproducible #1): Ask students to go back to this reproducible (page 17) and place the names of the two main characters—Henry and John—in their proper estates.

Joan of Arc

The Story of Her Life

Characters (in order of appearance):

NARRATORS 1-2

JOAN: the peasant girl who was to become the patron saint of France

HAUVIETTE: Joan's friend

ROBERT DE BAUDRICOURT: Governor of Vaucouleurs

JACQUES D'ARC: Joan's father

JEAN DE METZ: one of Baudricourt's squires

CHARLES: dauphin, then king, of France

CHURCHMAN

COUNT DUNOIS: one of Charles' loyal supporters

ARCHBISHOP OF REIMS

GUILLAME DE FLAVY: commander of Comiègne

BISHOP CAUCHON: a high-ranking French Bishop with English loyalties

ASSESSORS 1-3: priests at a church trial

PRIEST

❧ ACT I ❧

SCENE 1:

1425. A family garden in Donrémy, France.

NARRATOR 1: Thirteen-year-old Joan d'Arc was alone working in her father's garden when the church bells started ringing. Joan stopped what she was doing and fell to her knees to pray. As she did so, she saw a bright light and heard a voice coming from the direction of the church. She heard a voice tell her to be a good girl and to go to church often.

NARRATOR 2: Joan heard the voice identify itself as St. Michael. As Joan shaded her eyes from the light, she saw the royal patron saint. Joan felt as if she were in a dream and didn't hear her friend calling her.

HAUVIETTE: Joan, Joan. (*She sees her on the ground.*) Oh, there you are. Are you sleeping? I've been calling you.

NARRATOR 1: Joan looked up at her friend. Hauviette quickly stepped back.

HAUVIETTE: Your eyes! They are so bright! Have you got the fever?

JOAN (*smiling*): No, I am very well.

HAUVIETTE (*uncertain*): Are you sure?

JOAN: Yes.

HAUVIETTE: Then let us go play.

JOAN: No. I must go to church.

HAUVIETTE: You went this morning.

JOAN: I must go again.

NARRATOR 1: Joan went to church to thank God for St. Michael's visit. She did not know that she would receive many more visits from St. Michael, and from St. Catherine and St. Margaret, too.

SCENE 2:

Three years later. A secluded chapel in the woods near Donrémy.

NARRATOR 1: Joan was alone praying when she had another vision. She heard a voice telling her that she must drive the English out of France and bring the king to be crowned. The voice urged her to go, telling her that God would come to her aid.

NARRATOR 2: France was in the middle of a war with England (now called the Hundred Years War) that had been raging on and off for decades. The English were quickly gaining ground with the help of their ally, the Duke of Burgundy. And there was no strong leader to stop them.

NARRATOR 1: Before his death, the mad French king Charles VI signed a treaty passing the French crown not to his son, as was traditional, but to his daughter's son, instead. Since his daughter was married to the king of England, this meant that the French crown would one day pass to the king of England.

NARRATOR 2: The rightful heir, Charles VII, was known as the dauphin (eldest son of the king), and not the king because he was never crowned. This was due to the fact that Reims, where coronations had taken place for hundreds of years, was in enemy territory.

NARRATOR 1: At first, Joan did nothing, feeling she knew nothing of war. She also knew her parents would never let her leave. But the voices she heard became more and more insistent.

NARRATOR 2: Again, she heard a voice telling her to go to Vaucouleurs to see the governor, Robert de Baudricourt, and to ask him to send her to the rightful king.

SCENE 3:

Later that year. Inside the Governor's Mansion at Vaucouleurs.

NARRATOR: Joan found that she could no longer ignore the voices she heard. She ran away to Vaucouleurs and got Baudricourt to grant her an audience.

ROBERT DE BAUDRICOURT: What is it you wish?

JOAN: It is the will of my Lord that the dauphin be made king and have the realm in his command.

ROBERT DE BAUDRICOURT: Who is your lord?

JOAN: The King of Heaven.

ROBERT DE BAUDRICOURT (*laughing*): Is that so? (*to one of his men*) Take her home to her father. Tell him to box her ears.

NARRATOR: Joan went home feeling foolish and discouraged.

SCENE 4:

Fall, 1429. Back in Donrémy.

NARRATOR 1: After Joan returned home, much happened to make her even more aware of her country's need for help.

NARRATOR 2: In October, Burgundians attacked Joan's town of Donrémy. Although most of the town's inhabitants escaped unharmed, much of Donrémy was burned to the ground.

NARRATOR 1: At around the same time, the English laid siege to Orléans, one of the most important cities remaining in control of France.

NARRATOR 2: Joan's voices became more insistent than ever, this time urging her to

go and relieve the siege of Orléans.

NARRATOR 1: Joan's parents worried as their daughter kept more and more to herself. Joan's father spoke to her about his fears.

JACQUES D'ARC: I dreamed that you would go off with soldiers. If I thought such a thing could happen, I would drown you.

NARRATOR: Joan did not answer until her father had walked away.

JOAN (*softly*): Had I one hundred fathers and one hundred mothers, I still would go.

⚜ ACT II ⚜

SCENE 1:
Early 1429. Back in Vaucouleurs.

NARRATOR 1: Joan went back to Vaucouleurs.

JOAN: I have come to see Robert de Baudricourt.

JEAN DE METZ: He refuses to see you.

JOAN: Yet I must go to the king, even if I have to walk my feet off to my knees.

JEAN DE METZ: Is it not necessary that the king should be driven from the kingdom and that we should become English?

JOAN: No. But I must help him. My Lord wants me to.

JEAN DE METZ: Who is your lord?

JOAN: It is God.

NARRATOR 1: Joan's fierce belief won over the knight.

JEAN DE METZ (*placing his hand in Joan's*): I promise that, God willing, I will take you to the king. When do you want to go?

JOAN: Rather now than tomorrow. Rather tomorrow than later.

NARRATOR 1: Shortly thereafter, word of the girl from Donrémy reached the royal castle at Chinon. Charles sent for Joan.

NARRATOR 2: The people of Vaucouleurs gave Joan a tunic and leggings so that she could travel more comfortably. They also gave her a horse. Joan sat on this horse at the gates of Vaucouleurs. Joan, Jean de Metz, his squire, an archer, the royal messenger, and three servants were setting off to Chinon.

ROBERT DE BAUDRICOURT (*to Joan*): Are you not frightened? It is a long journey, and there are many enemy soldiers about.

JOAN: I am not afraid. God, my Lord, will clear the road for me to go to the dauphin. I was born for this.

ROBERT DE BAUDRICOURT: Go then, come what may.

NARRATOR 1: With those words, Joan and the others set off on their long journey to Chinon.

SCENE 2:
February, 1429. At the Royal Court in Chinon.

NARRATOR 1: Several days after her arrival, Joan was summoned to the court to meet the dauphin. He hid himself, but Joan went straight to him and fell to her knees.

JOAN: God give you life, gentle Dauphin.

CHARLES: How did you know me?

JOAN: I should know you well from all the others.

CHARLES: What is it you wish?

JOAN: I have come and am sent by God to

bring aid to you and your kingdom.

CHARLES: What will you do?

JOAN: I will raise the siege of Orléans. And I will take you to be crowned and consecrated in the city of Reims.

NARRATOR 1: For a king to be properly crowned, the French believed the ceremony had to take place at Reims, where the first Christian king of France had been crowned in 496.

NARRATOR 2: But Reims was deep in territory held by the English and the Burgundians. This made it difficult, if not impossible, for Charles to be crowned there.

CHARLES: How will you do these things?

JOAN: With the help of God. And you. I will need troops, arms, and horses.

CHARLES: I must talk to my advisers.

JOAN: Do not delay. You must use me quickly. I will last but a year, scarcely more.

NARRATOR 1: Charles' advisers suggested he send Joan to Poitiers to be investigated by learned men of the Church to make sure she was sent by God, not the devil.

SCENE 3:

March, 1429. At a hall in Poitiers.

NARRATOR 1: Joan sat in front of the churchmen at Poitiers.

CHURCHMAN: Do you know why you are here?

JOAN: Yes. But your questions waste valuable time.

CHURCHMAN: We must test you to learn....

JOAN (*interrupting*): I know not A from B,

but I come on behalf of the King of Heaven to raise the siege of Orléans and lead the dauphin to Reims for his coronation.

CHURCHMAN: Can you show us clear signs you are from God?

JOAN (*angry*): I have not come to Poitiers to make signs! Take me to Orléans and I will show you the signs for which I have been sent.

NARRATOR 1: The investigation dragged on for weeks. Finally, after much questioning and a thorough background search, the churchmen reached their conclusion.

CHURCHMAN: We pronounce Joan of Arc a good Christian and a good Catholic. The ready wisdom of her responses and the goodness of her life weigh in favor of her mission being a divine one.

NARRATOR 1: When Charles heard the commission's report, he gave Joan permission to prepare for battle.

NARRATOR 2: On April 27, 1429, Joan and an army of 4,000 marched for Orléans, led by a company of priests.

⚖ ACT III ⚖

SCENE 1:
May 4, 1429. Orléans.

NARRATOR 1: Joan was anxious to begin driving out the English from the moment she arrived in Orléans on April 29, but she was told by the army's officers to wait. She waited. Finally, on the afternoon of May 4, she jumped up from a nap and knew she could wait no more. She quickly called Jean de Metz.

JOAN: In God's name, my counsel has told

64

me I must attack the English.

NARRATOR 1: Joan and Metz quickly armed themselves, mounted their horses, and road to Orléan's Burgundy Gate. Joan held her battle standard high.

NARRATOR 2: As they road, they passed many wounded Frenchmen running back to the city. Without telling Joan, the French army had launched a surprise attack on the English fort of St. Loop. The attack had gone poorly, however, and the French army was in full retreat as Joan and Metz approached the fort.

JEAN DE METZ: It appears the French have already lost this battle.

NARRATOR 1: Joan held her standard higher.

JOAN: Not yet. (*shouting*) Turn back in the name of the Lord.

NARRATOR 1: The French troops rallied when they saw Joan's banner. They cheered and turned back with a vengeance. The English quickly surrendered. It was the first time during the seven-month siege that the French had captured an English fort.

SCENE 2:
May 7, 1429. Outside Orléans.

NARRATOR 1: Joan got up before dawn to attend mass before setting out with the army to attack Les Tourelles (the little towers), the strongest English fort for miles around. She spoke with Jean de Metz before the battle.

JOAN: Keep close to me today, because I will have much to do, and I will be wounded above the heart.

NARRATOR 1: Joan was wounded, just as she had foretold, when an arrow pierced her shoulder. Many French had fallen, and the army was making little headway in capturing the fort. Several commanders wanted to end that day's fighting. Joan refused to quit.

JOAN: In the name of God, you will soon enter the fortress. Never doubt it.

NARRATOR 1: The soldiers hesitated.

JOAN: Rest for a while. Eat. Drink.

NARRATOR 1: The soldiers did as they were told. Joan, whose wound was dressed, found a quiet spot to pray. After 15 minutes, she came back and mounted her horse. She held her standard in her good arm and summoned the troops.

JOAN: Go boldly in the name of the Lord.

NARRATOR 1: The French troops stormed the towers of the fort with renewed energy. Les Tourelles was taken. The next morning, the English abandoned all the forts in the area. In just days, Joan helped end England's seven-month occupation of Orléans.

SCENE 3:
July 17, 1429. The Cathedral at Reims.

NARRATOR 1: After her victory at Orléans, Joan pursued the second goal her voices had given her: to take Charles to be crowned at Reims. It was a dangerous journey and, at first, Charles was reluctant to make it. Joan convinced him that God was on their side and they made the journey—as much military advance as royal procession—safely.

NARRATOR 2: Charles entered the huge Gothic cathedral amid the cheers of his people. He proceeded to the altar to kneel in front of the Archbishop. Joan, holding her standard high, stood by his side.

ARCHBISHOP: Do you, Charles, swear to

defend the Church, preserve your people, and govern them with justice and mercy?

CHARLES: I do.

NARRATOR 1: The Archbishop anointed Charles with sacred oil. Then he placed the royal crown on his head.

ARCHBISHOP: I now pronounce you king by the grace of God.

NARRATOR 1: Joan knelt before the king, embraced his legs, and wept.

JOAN: Gentle King, now is done God's pleasure. You are the true king and the kingdom of France belongs to you.

NARRATOR 1: The audience cheered and trumpets blared.

ACT IV

SCENE 1:

May 23, 1430. Compiègne.

NARRATOR 1: Things went downhill for Joan after Charles' coronation. She wanted to reclaim all of France for her king, but Charles wanted to wait and see what could be worked out diplomatically. He gave Joan very little support when she tried to reclaim Paris, and she lost the battle.

NARRATOR 2: Still, Joan's voices told her to continue her fight. And Joan listened to the voices she heard. She knew that while Charles waited, more and more of France was being lost. When Joan learned that the Burgundians had laid siege to Compiègne, a town that had always been loyal to Charles, she immediately gathered troops and went there.

GUILLAME DE FLAVY: Welcome! We have prayed for help. Duke Philip has just taken Margny, the town across the river.

JOAN: My men rode all night. After they rest, we will attack Margny, and drive the Burgundians back.

NARRATOR 1: Later that day, Joan led about 400 knights out the town's gate and over the drawbridge toward Margny. But the Burgundians saw them coming and called for reinforcements. As Burgundian forces poured in from all directions, the French began to panic and turn back towards Compiègne.

JOAN (*shouting*): Do not turn back! God is with us! We shall be victorious!

NARRATOR 1: Few heard or heeded Joan's words as they retreated back to Compiègne. Commander Flavy watched from his post inside the town as French knights poured back into the city, with Burgundians in hot pursuit.

GUILLAME DE FLAVY: Quick! Take up the drawbridge! Close the town's gates!

NARRATOR 1: Most of the French had made it safely back inside the town. But Joan, who as leader had taken the most dangerous position at the rear of the retreat, did not.

NARRATOR 2: An archer grabbed Joan's cloak and yanked her off her horse. She was captured. As Joan had told Charles, she had lasted less than a year.

SCENE 2:

February-May, 1431. Rouen, France.

NARRATOR 1: The English were delighted to learn of Joan's capture. While the French believed Joan was working with God, the English believed she was working with the devil. The English paid the Burgundians a kingly ransom of 10,000 francs to make Joan their prisoner.

66

NARRATOR 2: The English then turned Joan over to the local pro-English church to try her for witchcraft, among other things. They hoped the trial would get rid of Joan and make Charles look bad at the same time.

NARRATOR 1: Although church trials were usually held in Paris, Joan was ordered tried in Rouen, the most English city in France. She was thrown into a filthy prison cell in the English castle at Rouen.

NARRATOR 2: On the first day of her trial, Joan was brought before two judges and dozens of priests, called assessors. The chief judge was Bishop Cauchon.

BISHOP CAUCHON: Do you swear to tell the truth throughout the trial?

JOAN: Concerning most matters I will willingly swear to tell the truth.

BISHOP CAUCHON: *Most* matters? Not all?

JOAN: I have been told by my secret counsel to reveal my visions to nobody.

BISHOP CAUCHON (*angry*)**:** You must answer us fully and truthfully.

JOAN: I have a greater fear of displeasing my voices than I have of not answering you.

NARRATOR 1: Cauchon looked at the other judge, then decided to proceed.

BISHOP CAUCHON: Let us begin our questioning.

ASSESSOR 1: As a child, did you have a great desire to defeat the Burgundians?

JOAN: I had a great desire that my king should have his kingdom.

ASSESSOR 2: Does God hate the English?

JOAN: As for the love or hate God has for the English, I know nothing. But I know they will be driven out of France.

ASSESSOR 3: Why were you chosen to lead this fight?

JOAN: It pleased God to use a simple maid to drive out the King's enemies.

NARRATOR 1: The trial lasted for months. Cauchon and his supporters had trouble proving Joan was a witch. But, given Joan's independent spirit, they had no trouble finding a charge that would stick.

BISHOP CAUCHON: We believe your voices are evil.

JOAN: But they come from God.

ASSESSOR 1: Only a church official, inspired by God, is capable of determining the origin of such voices.

BISHOP CAUCHON: And we say yours come from the devil.

JOAN: But everything good I have done, I have done by command of the voices.

BISHOP CAUCHON: You say you owe submission to God. But do you believe you owe submission to God's church on earth?

JOAN: Yes. But God shall be served first.

NARRATOR 1: The churchmen found another example of her disobedience.

BISHOP CAUCHON: It is a crime against God for a woman to wear men's clothes.

JOAN: These clothes do not burden my soul.

BISHOP CAUCHON: You are disobeying your church when you wear those clothes.

JOAN: I am obeying my God.

BISHOP CAUCHON (*angry*)**:** You must submit to the decisions of the church!

JOAN: In my opinion, God and the church are one. Why do you make such difficulties?

NARRATOR 1: Of the twelve formal charges made against Joan, the most serious was that Joan would not submit to the church on earth, but to God only.

NARRATOR 2: After making the charges,

the churchmen tried to make Joan confess. But she would not say she was wrong, even when they took her to the castle's torture chamber.

NARRATOR 1: Joan did make one short-lived confession, when she was first shown a stake where she could burn if she did not recant. But Joan withdrew her confession within days, saying she was wrong to confess just because of her "fear of the fire."

NARRATOR 2: On May 28, 1431, Bishop Cauchon pronounced Joan a relapsed heretic and sentenced her to death.

SCENE 3:

May 30, 1431. The town square at Rouen.

NARRATOR 1: Shortly after dawn, Joan was taken in the executioner's cart to the town square. There, on a high platform that all could see, was a scaffold with a stake and wood ready for burning.

JOAN (*crying out*): Oh, I had rather be seven times beheaded than burned!

NARRATOR 1: Joan was led to a platform where Bishop Cauchon was waiting for her.

BISHOP CAUCHON: We cast you forth from the church as an infected limb and hand you over to secular justice.

JOAN: Bishop, I die through you.

BISHOP CAUCHON: You die because you returned to your former evil-doing.

NARRATOR 1: Joan fell to her knees to pray but was quickly seized by the executioner and tied to the stake.

JOAN (*pleading*): Will someone give me a cross?

NARRATOR 1: An English soldier quickly made a small cross out of sticks and handed it to Joan. She kissed it and held it to her breast.

JOAN: I ask one more thing. I wish to look at the crucifix from the church.

NARRATOR 1: One of the churchmen went to the church and brought back the crucifix. He held it high in front of Joan.

JOAN (*calling out*): Forgive me as I have forgiven you!

NARRATOR 1: Joan died crying out to her saints and her God.

AFTERWORD

NARRATOR 2: The English were finally forced out of most of France in 1553, 22 years after Joan's death. In 1556, the Pope declared Joan innocent and her trial null and void. And in 1920, the Roman Catholic church made Joan of Arc a saint.

THE END

Joan of Arc

Teaching Guide

Background

About the Play

Joan of Arc tells the life story the French national heroine who became a Roman Catholic saint. Much of the dialogue in the play is taken from historical records of her life. Because of the religous aspects of the story, you'll need to use discretion when reading the play with your class. You may want to focus exclusively on the historical elements of Joan of Arc's story and her connection to the Hundred Years War.

About Joan of Arc

Joan of Arc—or Jeanne d'Arc, as she was known in France—was born in 1412 in the

---

WORDS TO KNOW

archbishop: the religious head of a province, ranking after the pope and cardinals

assessor: an official who helps a judge

audience: an opportunity to be heard

battle standard: banner or flag

bishop: a clergyman ranking above a priest, below an archbishop

consecrated: inducted into office with a religious ceremony

counsel: advisors

dauphin: the eldest son of the king

heretic: one who disagrees with established church beliefs

relapsed: fallen back into a former worse state

secular: not religious

siege: a military blockade of a place to try to force it to surrender

squire: a knight's shield- or armor-bearer

submission: the act of agreeing to accept the authority of another

village of Donrémy. The peasant girl spent most of her early years helping on the family farm with her brothers and sisters and learning to be a devout Catholic. Like most peasants of her time, she did not go to school and did not know how to read or write.

When Joan was 13, she began having religious experiences in which she believed St. Michael, St. Catherine, and St. Margaret were talking to her. At first, these voices simply told her to be a good Catholic. But by the time she was 16, they were telling her that God had chosen her to drive the English out of France, where they had been fighting on and off for decades. They also told her to take Charles VII to be crowned at Reims.

Joan reluctantly went to Vaucouleurs to ask the military commander there for an escort to take her to Charles in Chinon. The commander, Robert de Baudricourt, laughed at Joan and sent her home. Joan was discouraged, but she kept hearing the voices. And they grew more insistent as reports of enemy activity became more alarming. Two events in the fall of 1428 helped Joan pay heed to her voices. First, Burgundians (French citizens who supported the English) attacked Joan's village of Donrémy. Although most of the villagers escaped to a nearby walled village for safety, the Burgundians destroyed much of the town, including Joan's sacred church. Then, the English laid siege to Orléans, one of the most important cities remaining in control of France.

By January, 1429, Joan was back in Vacouleurs. Although Baudricourt initially refused to see her, she told her story to anyone who would listen. She found many supporters, including Jean de Metz, one of Baudricourt's squires. Finally, word of this maid who wanted to save France reached the royal court at Chinon, and Charles sent for Joan.

Joan, now dressed in a man's tunic for easier traveling, set off with Jean de Metz and several others on the long journey to Chinon. They traveled hundreds of miles through enemy territory before they reached Chinon. Legend has it that Joan's voices helped her find Charles, who was hidden in the crowd at the Royal Court. The two spoke, and Joan convinced Charles that, with the help of God, she could save France. It is uncertain whether or not Joan gave Charles a sign to prove that she was sent by God. Some historians believe this to be so, but there is no clear record of it.

Charles supported Joan but his advisers were not ready to trust the future of France to a peasant girl. Upon their advice, Charles took Joan to the city of Poitiers where she was investigated by learned men of the church. After several weeks of investigation and interrogation, they pronounced Joan a good Christian and Catholic and said that she was indeed sent by God.

Charles gave Joan money, troops, horses, and supplies to go raise the siege of Orléans. On April 27, 1429, Joan set off for Orléans with an army of 4,000. Two of Joan's brothers joined her on her way to the city.

Joan, holding her standard high, led the army in several battles in Orléans. The combat was long and bloody, and Joan herself was wounded in the shoulder by an English arrow. Yet the French fought on. Within days, under Joan's leadership and inspiration, they ended England's seven-month siege of the city.

After the victory at Orléans, Joan convinced Charles to proceed with his coronation at Reims. This was no easy task, as Reims was in the part of France occupied by English and Burgundian troops. Yet Joan led Charles and his military escort safely through enemy territory, winning several major battles along the way. And Joan stood beside Charles when he was crowned at the cathedral. To Joan, Charles was now a true king. He was crowned at the cathedral where Clovis, the first Christian king of France, had been

crowned nearly 1,000 years earlier.

Now that Charles had been crowned, Joan wanted to press forward and reclaim all of France, especially the English-controlled Paris, for its rightful king. Charles, who hoped to work things out diplomatically rather than militarily, gave Joan only his half-hearted support when she set out to free Paris in September, 1429. The attempt failed.

Joan was captured in May, 1430, while trying to defend the loyal town of Compiègne from attack by the Burgundians. She was ransomed by the English, who had her tried by a group of French clergy who were sympathetic to the English.

Joan was accused of many crimes, the greatest of which was heresy. Joan remained loyal to her king, her beliefs, and herself throughout the trial. When faced with death by fire she recanted, but within days took her recantation back.

Joan of Arc was burned at the stake before a large crowd at the town square of Rouen on May 30, 1431. Her ashes were thrown into the Seine River.

Joan's family later pressed to have the charges against Joan dropped. In 1456, Pope Callistus II pronounced Joan innocent. In 1920, Pope Benedict XV declared Joan a saint.

About the Hundred Years War: This struggle between England and France for control of France was actually a succession of wars with intermittent truces and treaties. The war began in 1337. Initially, the English were very successful. By the time Joan of Arc first set off for Vaucouleurs in 1428, England had taken over much of northern France. Joan helped turn the war around with her defeat of the English at Orléans in 1429. The patriotism inspired by Joan, and her death, helped the French continue to win battles. The English were finally driven out of all but a small part of France in 1453, 22 years after Joan's death.

Making Connections

Responding to the Play

Both sides of the story: Ask students to think about how the French saw Joan compared with how the English saw her. Ask, how could one person be considered an agent of God by some and an agent of the devil by others? Discuss how different beliefs and goals can make people see the same thing differently. Ask students to try to think of other examples of people who were or are praised by some and disparaged by others (i.e., Susan B. Anthony, Galileo, Malcolm X, Christopher Columbus, etc.).

"The will to believe": Tell students that when Joan was asked at her trial how she knew it was St. Michael that spoke to her, she answered, "I had the will to believe it." Discuss with students what they think Joan meant by this. Ask students what Joan's voices gave her that helped her drive the English out of France and see Charles crowned king. How was Joan able to convince others to follow her? You might want to tell students that one of the only ways a female with strong beliefs regarding public events could make herself heard in the male-dominated society in which Joan lived was to claim some visionary experience or prophetic power.

A fair trial? Discuss Joan's trial with students. Do they think it was fair? Why or why not? Ask students what makes a fair trial. Remind students that Joan had two powerful groups against her—the English and the English-backed French clergy.

Extension Activities

A good look at leaders: Tell students that Joan of Arc was the first woman of the people to assume a leadership role. She was a great

leader, too. Joan, a peasant and a woman, got soldiers, captains, even a king to do what she wanted. Ask students what qualities Joan of Arc had that made her a good leader (self-confidence, courage, determination). Ask students what qualities they think are important in a leader. Then ask students to work together to make a leadership collage. The collage should show—in words and pictures—what makes a good leader. It may also show pictures of people the students believe to be good leaders.

A saint or a witch? Divide the class, telling half the students they are fifteenth-century French men and women and the other half they are fifteenth-century English men and women. Then ask each group to get together and make a list of arguments supporting the belief that Joan is a saint (the French) or that Joan is a witch (the English). Ask students to debate the issue and see if either side can convince the other of their beliefs.

Designing a standard: Tell students that Joan carried a personal battle standard—a banner on a long pole. This standard was specially designed for her before she set off for Orléans. Ask students to work together to design a personal standard for Joan of Arc. You might want to divide the class into small groups and have a design competition, in which other classes familiar with the story of Joan of Arc make the final selection. Then have students work together to make the standard, using white fabric and fabric paints or markers. When students have completed the project, tell them that Joan's actual standard had a picture of Jesus and two angels painted on white silk. How does this compare to the standard they made and designed?

It's about time: Ask students to make a time line of Joan's life, based on information from the play. More advanced students might be encouraged to do additional research on Joan of Arc's life to fill in the time line even further.

The Three Estates (Reproducible #1): Ask students to go back to this reproducible (page 17) and place the names of the main characters from this play—Joan of Arc, King Charles, and Bishop Cauchon—in their proper estates.

Map it out (Reproducible #2): Ask students to use this map when reading the play to find out where the major events in Joan's life took place. Ask them to pay particular attention to whether the events took place in territory loyal to Charles VII or territory loyal to England and Burgundy. As an extension, you may wish to have students calculate the distance Joan traveled on some of her most important journeys—from Donrémy to Vaucouleurs, from Vaucouleurs to Chinon, from Chinon to Orléans, and from Compiègne to Rouen, for instance.

Further Reading

For Students:
Beyond the Myth: The Story of Joan of Arc by Polly S. Brooks (Harper, 1990).

Name _____

Joan of Arc's France

This is how France looked during Joan of Arc's life. Look at the map and find where the major events in Joan's life took place.

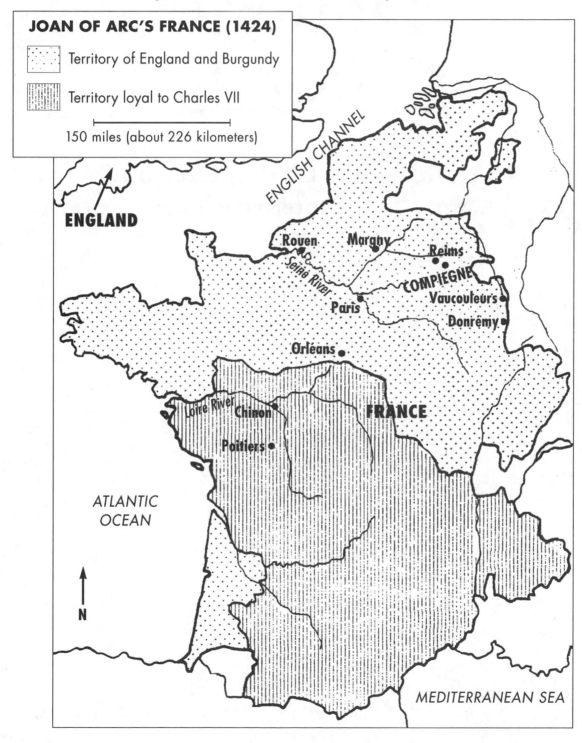

JOAN OF ARC'S FRANCE (1424)

- Territory of England and Burgundy
- Territory loyal to Charles VII

150 miles (about 226 kilometers)

ENGLISH CHANNEL

ENGLAND

Rouen •   Marghy •
Seine River   Reims •
COMPIEGNE
Paris •   Vaucouleurs •
Donrémy •
Orléans •

FRANCE

Loire River   Chinon •
Poitiers •

ATLANTIC OCEAN

N

MEDITERRANEAN SEA

Patient Griselda

"The Tale of the Clerk of Oxenford" from The Canterbury Tales

Characters (in order of appearance)

NARRATOR: Clerk of Oxenford

MAN 1-2
WOMAN 1-2 } people of Saluzzo

MARQUIS: a noble ruler

GRISELDA: a peasant girl

JANICULA: Griselda's father

ATTENDANT: the Marquis' assistant

DAUGHTER AND SON: (non-speaking roles)

❧ ACT I ❧

SCENE 1:

*The late Middle Ages. Outside a castle
in Saluzzo, Italy.*

NARRATOR: A strong, handsome young Marquis by the name of Walter ruled Saluzzo, a lovely plain in western Italy. The noble was a good ruler and was loved by all his people. Their only complaint was that he showed no interest in marriage. One day, a group of his people approached him with this complaint.

MAN 1: Oh, noble Marquis. We are heavy of heart.

MARQUIS: Why? Are you not happy with your lord?

MAN 1: We do not know how we could be happier, save for one thing.

MARQUIS: What is that?

MAN 1: We wish for you to take a wife.

MARQUIS: A wife? But why?

MAN 1: If you should die your lineage would cease. And woe to us should a stranger take your place.

MARQUIS (*moved*): I have enjoyed my liberty, dear people, but I trust your wisdom. Therefore I agree to marry, as soon as possible. (*The crowd cheers.*)

MAN 1: Then we will quickly find you the noblest and greatest wife in all the land.

MARQUIS: No. I will choose my own wife. And you must agree to worship and honor her, whoever she is, as if she were an emperor's daughter. (*The crowd quickly agrees.*) I pray now, speak no more of the matter.

MAN 1: Please, Lord, just tell us on what day this wedding will take place.

NARRATOR: The Marquis quickly set a date, whereupon his subjects fell upon their knees and thanked him.

SCENE 2:

The Marquis' wedding day.
In a village near his palace.

NARRATOR: There had been much preparation for the wedding. The Marquis had brooches and rings made for his bride-to-be. He had gowns made for her. His palace was made ready and filled with the best food from throughout Italy. Everything was ready, except for one thing. No one knew whom the Marquis planned to marry!

MAN 1: It is the day of the wedding, and our lord has not yet chosen a bride!

MAN 2: Has he deceived us?

WOMAN 1: Will he never wed?

NARRATOR: As they spoke, a procession, led by the Marquis, passed by.

WOMAN 2: It is the Marquis and his wedding party!

MAN 1: Look at their finery! The wedding will surely take place today. But who will be our lady?

NARRATOR: In this village lived a man named Janicula. He was considered the poorest man in the village except in one regard: He had a daughter, Griselda, who was rich in beauty and goodness. The Marquis had often seen her when he was out hunting or hawking. It was Griselda he intended to wed. The Marquis stopped at the door of her cottage just as Griselda was carrying in a bucket of water.

MARQUIS: Griselda.

NARRATOR: Griselda set down her water bucket and dropped to her knees. The Marquis got off his horse.

MARQUIS: Where is your father, Griselda?

GRISELDA: He is here, my lord.

NARRATOR: Janicula stepped outside. The Marquis took the old man by the hand and led him back into the humble cottage.

MARQUIS: Janicula, I can no longer hide the pleasure of my heart. If you allow it, my faithful servant, I will take your daughter for my wife.

JANICULA (*astounded*): Lord, my will is your will. Do as you think best.

MARQUIS: Then let us have a conference, just the three of us. You will be my witness when I ask Griselda to be my wife.

NARRATOR: The crowd wondered what was happening as the Marquis called for Griselda to join him and her father in the cottage.

MARQUIS: Griselda, it pleases your father and me that I should wed you. I hope that you also wish it so. But first I must ask you this question.

NARRATOR: Griselda stood pale and quiet as the Marquis spoke.

MARQUIS: Will you agree to do whatever I wish, even if it causes you pain, and never complain? If so, I will swear my allegiance to you.

GRISELDA (*trembling*): Lord, I am undeserving of your offer. But I will do as you wish. And I swear that I will never disobey you, even if it should kill me.

MARQUIS: That is enough, my Griselda.

NARRATOR: The Marquis walked out the door, followed by Griselda. He stopped to address the crowd.

MARQUIS: This is my wife that stands

76

here. Honor her and love her, I pray, all of you who love me.

NARRATOR: The Marquis asked his ladies to prepare Griselda for the wedding. They brushed her hair and replaced her rags with a beautiful wedding gown. Then the Marquis carried her off to his palace, where they celebrated until the sun went down.

❧ ACT II ❧

SCENE 1:

One year later. Inside the palace.

NARRATOR: The people celebrated when Griselda gave birth to her first child. They had quickly grown to love their new Marchioness and often praised the Marquis for his choice of wife. Listen to what the villagers had to say.

MAN 1: Our lord wedded with honor and good fortune.

MAN 2: A lady brought up in an emperor's hall could have no more grace than our Griselda.

WOMAN 1: And now she has given the Marquis a daughter. Perhaps a son will be next.

WOMAN 2: She is a good wife to the Marquis.

MAN 1: And more. She is a good mistress to her people.

NARRATOR: The Marquis clearly had nothing to prove to his people. But he felt he had something to prove to himself. Shortly after the birth of their daughter, the Marquis approached his wife in her chambers.

MARQUIS (*looking troubled*)**:** Griselda, do you remember the day I took you out of poverty and put you in a state of high honor?

GRISELDA: Yes, my lord.

MARQUIS (*lying*)**:** Though you are beloved to me, my people are unhappy to be the subjects of a peasant born into poverty. Since our daughter was born, they speak their unhappiness more openly. Since I desire to live my life in peace, I must do what is best for your daughter, what my people think is best.

NARRATOR: Griselda listened in silence, never questioning the truth of what her husband said.

MARQUIS: I ask that you now show me the patience and obedience that you swore to me in your village the day we were married.

GRISELDA (*quietly*)**:** Lord, my child and I are your own possessions. Do as you will.

NARRATOR: The Marquis was gladdened by Griselda's words, but pretended he was sad at what he had to do. He left his wife's room and instructed his most trusted attendant to go in and take the baby.

ATTENDANT: Madame, you must forgive me. The Marquis commands me to take this child.

NARRATOR: The attendant then snatched up the child as if he were taking her to be killed. Though Griselda loved her daughter, she neither wept nor sighed. But she spoke to the attendant.

GRISELDA: Please, may I kiss and bless my child before she dies. (*The attendant hands her back the child.*) Farewell, my child! I ask God to take your soul, for tonight you shall die for my sake.

NARRATOR: Griselda handed the child back to the attendant.

GRISELDA: Go now, and do as my lord wishes. But one thing I ask. Unless my lord forbids you, at least bury this child in

some place where neither animals nor birds will tear it to pieces.

NARRATOR: The attendant did not answer. He just walked away. When he found the Marquis, he reported Griselda's words and manner, which pleased the Marquis.

MARQUIS (*smiling*): Go now and take this child to my sister, the Countess of Panicia at Bologna. Tell her to raise her in gentleness and to hide whose child it is from all.

NARRATOR: The attendant did as he was told.

SCENE 2:

Four years later. In Griselda's chambers.

NARRATOR: After sending their daughter away, the Marquis watched his wife for signs of disloyalty. But she kept her promise. She never even spoke her daughter's name. Then Griselda gave birth to a son, and the people were delighted. But the Marquis still felt the need to test Griselda. He brought his lies to her again, when the boy was two years old.

MARQUIS: My people are especially unhappy since our son is born. They say, "When Walter is gone, the blood of Janicula shall succeed and be our lord." Their words break my heart. I must live in peace. So, as I did what was best for his sister, I must do what is best for him. I pray you be patient and not behave distractedly in your grief.

GRISELDA: As I left my clothing at home when I came to you, so I also left my will and my liberty. I took your clothing. I must accept your will.

NARRATOR: Again, the Marquis left with a sad face but a glad heart. Again, the attendant roughly took Griselda's child.

And again, Griselda asked to kiss and bless the child.

ACT III

SCENE 1:

Eight years later. In the Marquis' chambers.

NARRATOR: Over the years, the Marquis watched his wife closely but never heard a word of complaint from her. She remained as true and loyal to him as ever. And still he could think of nothing but testing her. When his daughter was twelve—of marrying age—he called once again on his loyal attendant.

MARQUIS: Please bring this message to the Pope in Rome. "I ask for permission to dissolve this marriage that has caused so much unhappiness among my people so that I may take another wife."

NARRATOR: The attendant took the Marquis' message to Rome. The Pope, not knowing that it was not the truth, sent a letter back with the attendant. It granted the Marquis the dispensation for which he asked.

MARQUIS (*smiling as he reads the letter*): Thank you. Now I bid you to go to my sister. Ask her to send my two children home in royal splendor.

ATTENDANT: Yes, my lord.

MARQUIS: Only it must be kept secret whose children they are. It should only be said that the maiden will soon wed the Marquis of Saluzzo.

ATTENDANT: Yes, my lord.

NARRATOR: The attendant carried his lord's message to Panicia. Shortly thereafter, in great magnificence and

78

joyful mood, the daughter and son, escorted by the Earl of Panicia and many lords, began their journey to Salerno.

SCENE 2:

One month later. In the palace's great hall.

NARRATOR: Griselda had heard rumors of her husband's decision to remarry, but he did not speak to her of it until the party from Panicia was just days away from the palace.

MARQUIS (*roughly*): Certainly, Griselda, I was pleased enough to have you for my wife. But my people want me to take another wife, and the Pope has consented to it.

GRISELDA: I never considered myself worthy in any way to be your wife. I have been and always shall be your humble servant. I will go, as you wish.

NARRATOR: Griselda left the palace and went home to live again with her father. Once there, she never spoke against the Marquis. Neither her words nor her face betrayed feelings of ill treatment.

SCENE 3:

Several days later. In the palace's great hall.

NARRATOR: The Earl of Panicia and his party arrived, and the Marquis welcomed them with much ceremony. He quickly sent for Griselda to be there, too.

MARQUIS (*pointing to their daughter*): Griselda, how do you like my new wife? Is she not beautiful?

NARRATOR: Griselda did not recognize her long-lost daughter in the beautiful and richly attired young lady before her.

GRISELDA: I have never seen anyone fairer, my Lord. (*She pauses.*) I only ask one thing of you.

MARQUIS: What is it?

GRISELDA: Please do not torment this maiden as you have done me. She was sheltered in her upbringing and could not endure as much as someone raised in poverty.

NARRATOR: When the Marquis saw this last example of Griselda's patience and good nature, he finally knew he need test her no more.

MARQUIS: This is enough, Griselda. I have thy faith and goodwill. I know it now. (*He takes Griselda in his arms and kisses her.*) Griselda, you are my wife. I have no other.

NARRATOR: Griselda looked as if she had woken from a dream.

MARQUIS: This is your daughter that you have just supposed to be my new wife. The other is your son, my heir. I secretly took them to Bologna. They are yours again. You have not lost your two children.

NARRATOR: Griselda fell in a swoon. Then she called both her children to her. They bathed in her tears as she embraced and kissed them.

GRISELDA: Oh, my dear children, my dear children. I thought cruel hounds or foul vermin had eaten you. But God, of His mercy, and your good father kept you.

NARRATOR: Griselda's ladies took her to her chambers. There they changed her out of her rags and into a gown of gold. Then they brought her back into the hall, where everyone honored her. They had a grand feast that day—grander even than that on their wedding day—that lasted until the stars shone in the sky. And the couple lived happily ever after, for the Marquis never tested Griselda again.

THE END

Patient Griselda
Teaching Guide

Background

About the Play

Patient Griselda is adapted from "The Clerk's Tale," one of twenty-four tales in Geoffrey Chaucer's The Canterbury Tales.

About Chaucer

Geoffrey Chaucer has been called the greatest medieval author, the first of the great English poets. He was the first author to use English in all his major works; before him, most literature intended for an educated audience was written in French or Latin.

Details of Chaucer's personal life are

WORDS TO KNOW

attendant: one who attends another to perform a service

clerk: a churchman

countess: the wife or widow of an earl or count, or a woman who holds one of those ranks

dispensation: a release from a vow or oath

earl: a nobleman who ranks below a marquis and above a viscount

marchioness: the wife or widow of a marquis or a woman who holds the rank of marquis

marquis: a nobleman who ranks below a duke and above an earl

noble: a person of high birth or rank

sketchy. He was born about 1340, the son of a vinter (wine merchant). He held positions at court under Edward III and Richard II, serving at home and abroad in war and peace. His work and travels took him to France, Italy, and Flanders.

During his life, he translated and wrote a number of stories and poems, the most famous of which is *The Canterbury Tales*. He also read stories, especially the works of such master poets and storytellers as Dante (1265-1321), Petrarch (1304-1374), and Boccaccio (1313-1375). Chaucer often used these masters' stories in his own works, translating them into his own language, often his own voice. This was an accepted practice during Chaucer's lifetime. Giving a story a wider audience was considered a good deed, not an act of plagiarism.

Chaucer spent the last years of his life in England. He died at his home in Westminster in 1400. Because he lived on the grounds of Westminster Abbey, he was buried in the south transept of the building. That spot is now known as Poet's Corner, and many other famous English poets have since been buried there.

About The Canterbury Tales

Chaucer's masterpiece, *The Canterbury Tales*, is a series of stories within a story written in verse. In it, Chaucer assembles thirty pilgrims at the Tabard Inn, near London, to travel 70 miles to the shrine of St. Thomas á Becket at Canterbury Cathedral. The choice of a pilgrimage as a framework—a popular device with writers of his day—allowed Chaucer to assemble a great variety of people who in any other setting would have had little or nothing to do with each other. Each pilgrim was supposed to tell two stories going to Canterbury, two stories coming home. With the thirty pilgrims, and two late additions, there should have been 124 stories. Chaucer never finished this work, however, and only

twenty-four tales exist, some of which are unfinished fragments.

Although written in Middle English, *The Canterbury Tales* is a timeless work. Chaucer's powers of observation; his humor; his intentional ambiguity; and his genial tolerance of humanity all combine to make *The Canterbury Tales* as true and entertaining today as it was when it was written six hundred years ago.

About "The Tale of the Clerk of Oxenford"

Chaucer based this tale on a story by the Italian poet Petrarch. Most scholars agree that the tale deals chiefly with ideals of Christian behavior, not marriage. "The Clerk's Tale" is a religious allegory showing the importance of submission, loyalty, and goodness above all.

The religious bent of the story becomes clearer to modern-day readers when they realize that the teller of the tale, the Clerk of Oxenford, is a churchman. In the Middle Ages, the word "clerk" meant "churchman." At that time, churchmen were among the few who were educated enough to do clerical jobs.

Making Connections

Responding to the Play

The story behind the story: Point out to students that a clerk in the Middle Ages was a churchman, and explain that most scholars think "The Clerk's Tale" is allegorical—that it has hidden spiritual meaning. Also remind students that during the Middle Ages, the church was very powerful and influential. Discuss with students what values they think the story is trying to teach.

Then and now: Ask students why they think Griselda was so obedient to the Marquis. Point

out that in the Middle Ages, women had to obey their husbands, their fathers, and their lords; and peasants had to obey their lords. Ask students to compare the marriage of the Marquis and Griselda to a marriage today. Ask them to look at such things as class distinctions, the role of parents in agreeing to a marriage, and the relationship between husband and wife.

Fool or hero? Ask students if they think Griselda was a fool or a hero for being so patient with the Marquis. Ask if they think their opinions of Griselda would differ from those held by people six hundred years ago. If so, why? If students were to write a modern day version of the tale, what would they change? How would Griselda behave?

Extension Activities

Frame it! Explain to students that *The Canbterbury Tales* has a frame story structure—it is a collection of stories told within the framework of a pilgrimage. Ask students to brainstorm a frame they might use for a collection of stories written by the class. These could include a class field trip, a class sleepover, or any other event when the entire class is thrown together for an extended period of time. Once students have agreed upon the frame, ask each student to write a story to include within the frame. When everyone is done, read the stories aloud. Then collect them and collate them into a class book. As in *The Canterbury Tales*, you might want to write an introduction—or appoint one or more students to do so—that establishes the frame and introduces each student.

Pilgrimage: Ask students to find Great Britain on a world map. Then ask them to find London and Canterbury, to see where Chaucer's Pilgrims traveled. Next, ask students to look at a map of their own state. Ask them to find a

place they might like to visit that is within a 70-mile radius—the distance from London to Canterbury Cathedral—of their home town. Point out to students that although they would probably make their trips by car in a matter of hours, most of Chaucer's pilgrims either walked or rode a horse on their journey, which lasted many days. Challenge students to map out the route they would use to get there. Then have them calculate how many days it would take to walk the 70 miles and how long it would take to get there by car.

Family trees: Tell students that family names were very important during the Middle Ages. Ask students to make a family tree for Griselda and the Marquis that includes all the related characters in the play. Then ask students to make their own personal family trees going back at least to their grandparents, and further, if possible.

The Three Estates (Reproducible #1): Ask students to go back to this reproducible (page 17) and place the names of the main characters from this play—Griselda and the Marquis—in their proper estates.

Further Reading

For Students:

Canterbury Tales by Geoffrey Chaucer (Lothrop, 1988).

A Taste of Chaucer by Anne Malcolmson (Harcourt, 1964).

A Medieval Feast by Aliki. (Harper, 1983).

Sir Gawain and the Green Knight

A King Arthur Legend

Characters (in order of appearance):

NARRATOR

KING ARTHUR

GREEN KNIGHT

SIR GAWAIN: one of King Arthur's knights

QUEEN GUINEVERE: King Arthur's wife

PORTER: doorman at the castle

LORD: lord of the castle in the woods

LADY: wife of the castle's lord

GUIDE

ACT I

SCENE:
New Year's Day, mid-1400s. At Camelot, King Arthur's palace.

NARRATOR: King Arthur, Queen Guinevere, and many noble knights and ladies were celebrating the new year at Camelot. The servants brought out the food and all were seated to eat, save King Arthur.

KING ARTHUR: I cannot eat until I hear of or see some stirring adventure.

NARRATOR: Guinevere smiled at Arthur. She was familiar with this habit of his.

KING ARTHUR: Does not anyone here have an exciting event to share with me?

NARRATOR: As if in answer, there came a commotion at the entrance to the hall. All looked and gasped in horror at what they saw: A giant, green man on a great green horse.

QUEEN GUINEVERE: My lord!

NARRATOR: Arthur, studying the stranger and his stallion, said not a word.

GREEN KNIGHT (*bellowing*)**:** Where is the governor of this gathering?

NARRATOR: Arthur stepped forward.

KING ARTHUR (*fearless*)**:** Sir Knight, welcome to Camelot. I am Arthur, head of the household. Pray tell me what you wish.

GREEN KNIGHT: Your praises are sung far and wide. If you and your knights are so bold and brave as men tell, you will grant the game I ask of you.

KING ARTHUR: What game shall I give you?

READ ALOUD PLAYS: SIR GAWAIN AND THE GREEN KNIGHT
Scholastic Professional Books, 1998

NARRATOR: The Green Knight held up a huge ax.

GREEN KNIGHT: I wonder if there are any so hardy here in this house that will exchange with me one strike for another.

KING ARTHUR: Who is to take the first blow?

GREEN KNIGHT: I will. Provided that I may give one in return in a year's time.

NARRATOR: The stranger stared at the men in King Arthur's court, waiting to see who would accept his challenge. After a few minutes, he shook his huge head in disgust.

GREEN KNIGHT (*laughing loudly*): Is this truly Arthur's house, renowned for fierceness and fearlessness?

NARRATOR: Arthur, refusing to be shamed, quickly spoke up.

KING ARTHUR: Your loud words do not frighten us. You have spoken in folly, and you will get as you deserve. Give me your ax.

NARRATOR: The Green Knight dismounted from his horse and handed Arthur his ax. Meanwhile, Arthur's nephew, who had been seated beside the beautiful queen, rose and spoke to Arthur.

SIR GAWAIN: My lord, let me take thy place. My life, if lost, would be least missed.

NARRATOR: Arthur talked this over with his court. They advised him to accept Gawain's proposal. Arthur called his nephew to his side and handed him the ax.

KING ARTHUR: Son of my sister, teach this man his lesson with one cut.

NARRATOR: Sir Gawain approached the Green Knight.

GREEN KNIGHT: Let us tell our agreement, sir knight, before we go further.

SIR GAWAIN: I, Gawain, will strike thee now. You will have a turn with me in twelve months time.

GREEN KNIGHT: I am pleased, Sir Gawain, that you who understand should strike this blow.

SIR GAWAIN: Tell me, where will I find thee in a twelvemonth?

GREEN KNIGHT: I will tell you after I have taken the blow.

QUEEN GUINEVERE (*whispering*): I pray that he is unable to do so.

NARRATOR: The Green Knight kneeled and rested his great head on the ground. He lifted his green hair to lay his green neck bare.

GREEN KNIGHT: I am ready.

NARRATOR: Sir Gawain raised the ax and struck straight through the Green Knight's neck, causing his head to roll across the floor.

QUEEN GUINEVERE: Surely he is dead! Gawain is free from the bargain.

NARRATOR: But much to the queen's—and the entire court's—horror, the Green Knight ran across the room and picked up his head. Then he hopped on his horse and held his head so that its eyes met Gawain's.

GREEN KNIGHT: Get ready, Gawain, to do as you promised. Go north to the Green Chapel. You have earned a sharp blow next New Year's day.

NARRATOR: With those words, the headless Green Knight galloped off. Arthur, having met a marvel, sat down to eat, beckoning Sir Gawain to come eat at his side.

⚜ ACT II ⚜

SCENE 1:

The following November. At Camelot.

NARRATOR: A year slipped swiftly past. After feasting All Saint's Day, Sir Gawain knew it was time to head north.

SIR GAWAIN: My lord and uncle, I must beg your leave. I must set forth in the morning to answer my part of last New Year's bargain.

KING ARTHUR: I grant you leave, good Gawain. May God guide you to the Green Knight and safely home again.

NARRATOR: Gawain rose early the next morning and heard Mass. Then, dressed in his shining knight's armor, he took leave of King Arthur and his court.

KING ARTHUR: God be with you.

SIR GAWAIN: Farewell.

NARRATOR: Gawain mounted his groomed horse, Gringolet. He took his shield with its five-pointed star, or pentangle. It was proof that Gawain possessed the five virtues: fellowship, nobility of mind, courtesy, restraint, and obedience to God. Then Gawain spurred his horse and sped away.

SCENE 2:

The next eight weeks. North of Camelot.

NARRATOR: Gawain rode through cold, snow-covered forests and over icy hills. Everywhere, he asked the same question.

SIR GAWAIN: Do you know of the Green Knight, or the Green Chapel?

NARRATOR: Always the answer was the same: no. Gawain prayed for guidance as Gringolet galloped on. When Gawain hadn't yet found the chapel on Christmas Eve, he prayed harder than ever.

SIR GAWAIN (*on his knees*): Please give me some place where I might hear Mass tomorrow, on Christmas day.

NARRATOR: Sir Gawain got back on Gringolet and had not traveled far before he saw a palace through the trees.

SIR GAWAIN (*taking off his helmet*): Thank you. My prayers are answered.

NARRATOR: Gawain galloped to the castle's gated entrance.

SIR GAWAIN (*calling*): Greetings!

NARRATOR: A porter hurried to the gate.

SIR GAWAIN: Good sir, will you go ask your lord if I may stay and pray here?

NARRATOR: The porter rushed off but quickly returned and opened the gate.

PORTER: You are most welcome here.

NARRATOR: Sir Gawain rode his horse inside the gates. Servants hurried out to stable his horse; lords and ladies came out to welcome Gawain. They escorted him into a huge hall, where the lord awaited him by a roaring fire.

LORD: I welcome you, Sir Knight, to dwell here as you wish.

SIR GAWAIN: I give you my great thanks.

NARRATOR: The men embraced. Then the lord brought Gawain to a chamber where he was stripped of his cold, wet garments and dressed in warm, rich robes.

LORD: Come now. You must eat.

NARRATOR: The lord led Gawain back to the great hall, where a fantastic feast was awaiting him. As Gawain ate, the lord asked him his name.

SIR GAWAIN: I am Gawain, of King Arthur's court.

LORD: Sir Gawain! I am very glad you are my guest for Christmas. I have heard much that is good about you.

NARRATOR: After Gawain had eaten his fill, the lord led him to his chapel to hear Mass. His lady joined them, along with a very ugly old woman whom Gawain later learned was Morgan the Fay.

LORD (*to his wife*): My love, this is Sir Gawain, nephew of King Arthur of the Round Table. He will be our guest for Christmas.

LADY (*smiling*): Welcome, Sir Gawain.

NARRATOR: Sir Gawain answered her smile. As he did, he thought to himself that he had never seen anyone of greater beauty, not even his queen, Guinevere.

SCENE 3:

Three days later. At the castle's great hall.

NARRATOR: The Christmas celebration was a long one. On the third day, Gawain's thoughts turned to the reason he was away from Camelot.

SIR GAWAIN: My lord, you have been so good to me, I am sorry to go. But I must leave on the morrow.

LORD: Your presence brings me such pride and pleasure. I do not wish to see you go. What drives you away during the holidays?

SIR GAWAIN: I must find the Green Chapel by New Year's morning. I agreed to a tryst there. And I have but three full days to find it if I leave on the morrow.

LORD (*laughing*): If that is it, then you must stay! The Green Chapel is hardly two miles from here. You shall be shown your way there on New Year's morn.

SIR GAWAIN (*relieved*): My goal is gained! I thank you a thousand times. I will gladly stay on here, and do as you wish.

NARRATOR: The lord thought for a few moments.

LORD: You must stay and rest to recover from your long travels. My wife will keep you company at my castle each day while I take my other guests hunting.

SIR GAWAIN: Whatever you wish, I will do as you ask.

LORD: One thing more. Let us agree that whatever I win in the wood shall be yours, and whatever you harvest in my household you will give in return.

SIR GAWAIN (*smiling*): I agree to that.

LORD: Let us drink our wine to seal the bargain!

ACT III

SCENE 1:

The following day, December 29. Inside Sir Gawain's room.

NARRATOR: While Gawain slept, the lord and many of his guests got up early for the hunt. Gawain was finally wakened by the sound of his door opening. He peeked through the bed curtain and saw the lady of the house stealing into his room. He closed his eyes to feign sleep, but opened them wide when the lady sat on the bed beside him.

LADY: Good morning, Sir Gawain! You are a careless sleeper if one can creep up on you so!

SIR GAWAIN: Good morning, gracious lady.

NARRATOR: Sir Gawain was in an awkward position. It would be rude of him to ask his hostess to leave. Yet it was unseemly for him to entertain her alone in his room.

SIR GAWAIN: If you would grant me leave, lovely lady, I would dress myself to better entertain you.

LADY: Nay, fair sir. Do not budge from your bed. I want to speak with my prisoner.

NARRATOR: Sir Gawain laughed at the lady's description of him.

LADY: Sir Gawain, you are praised by all. Now we are alone, I offer you my praises.

SIR GAWAIN (*embarrassed*)**:** I am an unworthy knight, madam.

LADY: Nay! If I were to choose a husband anew, no lord alive would I want before you.

SIR GAWAIN: In truth lady, you did better. But I am proud of the praise you give me.

NARRATOR: They went on like this for some time, with the lady professing her love for Sir Gawain, and the knight politely rebuffing her. Finally, the lady rose from the bedside.

LADY (*flirtatious*)**:** I will leave now. But I can hardly believe you are truly Gawain, prince of chivalrous love and virtue.

GAWAIN (*upset*)**:** Why? Have I offended you in some way?

LADY: Surely, that knight would crave at least one kiss out of courtesy.

GAWAIN: If a kiss is what you wish, it is my courtly duty to obey.

NARRATOR: The lady leaned over and kissed Gawain on the cheek.

SCENE 2:
That evening. In the castle hall.

NARRATOR: The host called for Gawain when he returned from the hunt.

HOST (*pointing to a pile of deer carcasses*)**:** How do my spoils please you?

SIR GAWAIN: Truly, this is the finest venison I have seen in seven winters.

HOST: I give all to you, Gawain, according to our agreement.

SIR GAWAIN: And I gladly give you what I've gained, sir, a kiss.

NARRATOR: Sir Gawain kissed him.

LORD (*smiling*)**:** Thank you. Now, tell me, where did you win that wealth?

SIR GAWAIN: I will not tell. That was not part of our agreement.

NARRATOR: They laughed and went off to dinner, promising to keep the agreement for another day.

SCENE 3:
The next morning. In Gawain's room.

NARRATOR: Again, Gawain slept while the lord and his company went off to hunt. And, again, he was awakened when his hostess came in his room and sat upon his bed.

SIR GAWAIN: Good morning, lady.

LADY: Good morning, Gawain, if that is who you truly are.

SIR GAWAIN: What do you mean?

LADY: Have you forgotten what I taught you yesterday? If you were a true knight, you would have claimed a kiss already.

SIR GAWAIN: I shall kiss at your command.

NARRATOR: The lovely lady leaned over and kissed him. Then, as she did the day before, she tried to woo the good Gawain.

LADY: You are known as the most noble knight. Since my lord and master is out in the woods, far away, surely you could teach me about love.

NARRATOR: Sir Gawain thought quickly.

SIR GAWAIN: My lady, it is you who could teach about love. You are much more skilled than I.

NARRATOR: The lady laughed. Then she continued testing and trying him, tempting him to sin. But, careful not to offend her, he continued to refuse. Finally, the lady gave up.

LADY: I must go now. But I will kiss you again.

NARRATOR: The lady kissed Gawain for the second time that day and left.

SCENE 4:

That evening. In the castle hall.

NARRATOR: The host greeted Gawain and presented him with the huge head of the boar he had hunted and killed that day.

HOST: What think you of my hunting skills now?

SIR GAWAIN: Never have I seen so big a boar!

HOST: It is yours, as we agreed.

SIR GAWAIN: And here are my winnings.

NARRATOR: Sir Gawain clasped his host's neck and kissed him twice.

HOST: Two kisses!

SIR GAWAIN: Yes, and now we are quits.

HOST: Until the morrow.

SCENE 5:

The next morning. In Gawain's room.

NARRATOR: For the third time, Gawain slept while his host went off to hunt. And, also for the third time, the lady crept into Gawain's room while he was sleeping. The good knight, in a deep dream about the Green Knight, did not hear her enter.

LADY: How can you sleep on such a beautiful morning?

NARRATOR: Sir Gawain shook his head as he crept up from the depths of his dream. The lady laughed and kissed him.

SIR GAWAIN: Good morning, fair lady.

LADY: You call me fair lady, yet you do not love me.

NARRATOR: Sir Gawain knew not what to say. He did not want to be discourteous to his hostess. Yet he also did not want to sin or deceive his host.

LADY: Is there someone you love better?

SIR GAWAIN: I have no beloved yet and I wish for none.

LADY (*upset*)**:** Those words hurt me more than any could. Give me now a gracious kiss and I will quickly depart.

NARRATOR: The lady quickly kissed Gawain, but could not yet bring herself to leave.

LADY: Dear knight, do me this pleasure. Give me something of yours to comfort me. Even your glove will help me remember you when you are gone.

SIR GAWAIN (*shaking his head*)**:** How can I give you a glove, you who deserve the loveliest thing I possess? Yet, alas, I came on this journey with no gifts to give.

LADY: Noble knight, though I have nothing

of yours, I still wish to give a gift to you.

NARRATOR: The lady took off a rich ruby ring and held it towards Gawain.

SIR GAWAIN: Nay. I will have no gifts from you as I have none to give in return.

LADY: Do you refuse this ring because it is too rich? Take then this silk belt I wear.

NARRATOR: The lady unbound a green embroidered silk belt from around her hips.

SIR GAWAIN: My lady, please. I cannot take any gift when I have none to give.

LADY (*ignoring him*)**:** Is this belt too poor for you? It may not look as valuable as the ring, but it is even more so. Whoever wears it close about him will be kept safe from harm.

NARRATOR: Sir Gawain then thought how the belt would help him in his match. When the lady pressed the belt upon him a second time, he did not refuse it.

LADY: Remember me by it, and keep it always. But do not tell my husband I gave it to you, for it would anger him.

NARRATOR: The lady then kissed Gawain a third time and left.

SCENE 6:
That evening. In the castle hall.

NARRATOR: When the lord returned from the hunt Gawain joyously greeted him.

SIR GAWAIN: I will be first to pay tonight!

NARRATOR: Then Gawain clasped the lord's neck and kissed him three times.

LORD: Three kisses! All I have got for you is this fox's pelt.

SIR GAWAIN: It is enough. Thank you.

NARRATOR: The two men went off to dine. Not a word was said about the silk belt.

☙ ACT IV ☙

SCENE:
The next morning. Outside the castle.

NARRATOR: Sir Gawain, astride his horse Gringolet, left the castle early the next morning. The knight wore full armor. And underneath it, wrapped around his hips, he wore the green silk belt. A guide from the castle rode beside him into the deep, dark forest.

GUIDE: Let us stop here, sir.

SIR GAWAIN: Have we reached the Green Chapel?

GUIDE: No, though we are near that notorious place.

SIR GAWAIN: Let us go forth to find it then.

GUIDE: Nay. Pray listen to what I say. You are a lord I love dearly. I do not wish to see you harmed. Yet the man you go to see is monstrous. He shows no mercy.

SIR GAWAIN: But I said I would meet him this day a twelvemonth ago.

GUIDE: Please, Sir Gawain, go away without seeing him. I will keep secret your flight.

SIR GAWAIN: I thank you for seeking to save me, but I cannot flee in fear. To do so would make me a coward.

GUIDE: If you wish to lose thy life, I cannot stop you. But I will not go one step further.

SIR GAWAIN: Tell me, then, where is the Green Chapel?

GUIDE: Take this same rough track to the bottom of the valley. You will soon see the Green Chapel you seek.

SIR GAWAIN: Thank you.

GUIDE: God go with you, noble Gawain.

NARRATOR: The guide turned and galloped away while Gawain followed the track down the dark, overgrown valley. He looked all around until he spotted a green mound over a hollow cave. He rode over to it.

SIR GAWAIN (*loudly*): If this is the Green Chapel, where is the master of this place? It is Gawain, come to meet him.

NARRATOR: Gawain heard a loud grinding noise, like the sharpening of an ax. Then the Green Knight came out of the cave carrying a huge gleaming ax.

GREEN KNIGHT: Welcome to my place, Gawain. You have kept your agreement. Now take off your helmet and have your payment. And give no argument, as I gave none.

SIR GAWAIN: I will do as you ask.

NARRATOR: Gawain took off his helmet and bravely bent his head. The Green Knight then lifted his ax and swung. As he did so, Gawain glanced up and cringed at what he saw. The giant jerked back the blade.

GREEN KNIGHT: Such cowardice! Are thee truly Gawain, who never showed fear?

SIR GAWAIN: I flinched once. I will not flinch again.

NARRATOR: The Green Knight hoisted his ax once again. This time he let the ax fall hard. But he let it fall, not on Gawain, but on the ground next to the good knight.

GREEN KNIGHT: Ho! Ho! Now I have your attention. I shall strike my hardest!

NARRATOR: The Green Knight lightly lifted his weapon and let it fall. But he guided it so that it just nicked the knight's neck. Gawain quickly jumped to his feet.

SIR GAWAIN: Enough! I have taken my blow. If you continue, I will match you blow for blow.

NARRATOR: The Green Knight leaned on his ax and smiled at Gawain.

GREEN KNIGHT: Do not be so fierce, fearless knight. I will strike thee no more. You gave me all your winnings, except for the green silk belt, and for that I just nicked you.

NARRATOR: Sir Gawain looked towards his hips, where the belt remained well hidden.

GREEN KNIGHT: I also know of thy kisses and thy courteous ways with my wife.

SIR GAWAIN (*confused and upset*): *Your* wife?

GREEN KNIGHT: Yes. I planned her visits to you myself.

SIR GAWAIN (*in disbelief*): *You* sent her to me?

GREEN KNIGHT: Yes. I sent her to test you. And you seem truly a most faultless knight. Your first two blows were intended misses, for the two promises you kept, the exchange of kisses.

SIR GAWAIN: And the third blow?

GREEN KNIGHT: You did fail on the third day. You did not give me the green belt you wear, though it belongs to me. For that you spilled some blood.

SIR GAWAIN (*ashamed*): I confess, sir. I was wrong to accept the belt. I am at fault.

GREEN KNIGHT: Your loyalty to your host was not total, but that was not for wickedness or wooing. Rather, it was for love of your life, which is less blameworthy.

NARRATOR: Sir Gawain took off the belt and flung it at the Green Knight's feet.

SIR GAWAIN: Forgive me. Let me gain your grace anew.

GREEN KNIGHT: You have acknowledged your mistake. You are forgiven. But keep the belt that is green like my gown so that you may always remember this contest.

SIR GAWAIN: I will take this belt to remind me of my failing.

NARRATOR: Sir Gawain picked up the belt.

SIR GAWAIN: Now tell me, if you please, your true name.

GREEN KNIGHT: I am Bertilak. Morgan the Fay, the old woman you saw at the castle, used the magical arts she learned from Merlin to transform me into what you see.

SIR GAWAIN: Why did she do so?

GREEN KNIGHT: She wanted to test the reputation of the knights of the Round Table.

SIR GAWAIN (*hanging his head*): And I have failed.

GREEN KNIGHT: Nay, you are a true knight. I have met none truer. Now come back to my home and we will celebrate the new year.

SIR GAWAIN: No, I must return to Camelot. (*He pauses.*) Please commend me to your wife, and beg her to forgive me.

GREEN KNIGHT: I will, good Gawain, I will.

NARRATOR: The two men exchanged kisses and went their separate ways. Gawain returned to Camelot. Arthur was delighted to see Gawain again. He listened to Gawain's story and was proud of how the knight handled his task. But Gawain took little comfort in Arthur's praise. He felt he had failed.

THE END

Sir Gawain and the Green Knight

Teaching Guide

Background

About the Play

This play is based on the poem *Sir Gawain and the Green Knight*, which critics call one of the great masterpieces of medieval literature in general and Arthurian writing in particular. The poem, written by an unknown author in about 1375, is a romantic tale about King Arthur's nephew, Sir Gawain. In the story, Gawain is courageous and constant in the face of terror and temptation. He emerges from a series of tests as the model of knighthood.

The 2,531-line poem has an alliterative meter, in which two or more words in one line have the same initial sounds, and was written during what is now known as the Alliterative Revival of the fourteenth century. (Alliterative poems had been very popular in the centuries before the Norman Conquest.) It was written in Middle English in the regional dialect of the West Midlands.

The language, though rich and colorful, was considered less accessible by Londoners and others in the populous Southeast England at the time. As a result, the poet never had a fraction of the audience that, for instance, his contemporary Chaucer had.

Like Chaucer, the poet combined borrowed and original material in his work. The story's beheading game was borrowed from an eighth- or ninth-century Irish legend. The temptation of the knight's chastity dates back to early French romances.

WORDS TO KNOW

All Saint's Day: a Christian feast celebrated on November 1 in honor of all saints

chivalrous: marked by honor, generosity, and courtesy, especially to women

knight: a nobleman and soldier

porter: a doorman

The author tied these together with what appears to be an original idea, the exchange of the winnings.

There is only one existing early manuscript of *Sir Gawain and the Green Knight*, and it is in the British Museum. The poem, along with three others believed to be by the same author, is written in fourteenth- or early-fifteenth-century hand on velum.

About the Author

J.R.R. Tolkien, in the introduction to his translation of *Sir Gawain and the Green Knight*, says "educated men of the fourteenth century were shockingly incurious about authors as persons." As a result, all that is known about the author of *Sir Gawain and the Green Knight* is what can be learned from the existing manuscript and the four poems contained in it. For example, based on his description of dress, the author, now generally known as the "Gawain poet," was probably writing in the late 1300s. His descriptions of life at court and the hunt show that he was well acquainted with courtly life. That, combined with his knowledge of Latin and French, make it likely that he was a member of the gentry. And his dialect places him in the West Midlands—Lancashire or somewhere farther north.

About the Arthurian Legends

Poets and writers have been telling stories about King Arthur for almost one thousand years. No one knows if these stories have any basis in fact, if there ever was a real Arthur. Scholars say that, if there was, he lived in the sixth or seventh century, may or may not have been of royal blood, and was an acclaimed hero and leader. Whether fact or fiction, the legend of King Arthur was first transmitted orally and later written down by many great authors, including the author of *Sir Gawain*

and the Green Knight. In nearly all the retellings, Arthur is shown as a defender of the faith and the ruler of a kingdom based on law and order. His nephew, Sir Gawain, one of the greatest of his knights, appears in many of the stories. As in *Sir Gawain and the Green Knight*, Gawain is famous for his courtesy and bravery, and is always successful in his quests.

Making Connections

Responding to the Play

The moral of the story is…: Ask students what morals they find in this story. Discuss loyalty, bravery, and honesty. You might ask students if they know any stories—old or contemporary— that contain similar morals. For example, if students have read *The Song of Roland*, they might compare and contrast Roland and Gawain.

Testing, one, two, three: Ask students to think about the three tests Gawain's host put to him. Ask, what made Gawain pass the first two tests? (his determination not to sin or betray his host) What made him fail the third test? (his love of life) Ask students if they think they would have passed the third test. Why or why not?

Success or failure? Ask students whether they think Gawain proved himself to be a true knight in this story. Why or why not? Who in the story shares their belief? (Arthur, his court, and the Green Knight think Gawain succeeded; Gawain thinks he failed.)

All about Arthur: Ask students what they know about the legend of King Arthur. Discuss what virtues King Arthur and the Knights of the Round Table are known for. Then ask students what, if anything, they have ever heard about Sir Gawain. Explain that the play

is one of the many King Arthur legends written over the past one thousand years.

Extension Activities

A little alliteration: Tell students that the original *Sir Gawain and the Green Knight* is an alliterative poem. Explain that alliteration is the repetition of the initial consonant sounds in two or more neighboring words or syllables (as in *creepy crawlers* in *deep, dark drawers*). Then tell students they are going to write an alliterative poem together. Choose a topic, then ask for a volunteer to write the first line of the poem, using alliteration. Then ask for volunteers to continue adding alliterative lines to the poem, making sure to call on everyone in class. You might want to print your poem and share it with other classes.

Picture perfect: Ask each student to imagine what the Green Knight looks like, then to draw a picture of him. Then ask students to imagine that they are publishers about to print a copy of *Sir Gawain and the Green Knight*, and ask them to select the drawing they think they would use on the cover of their books. Discuss why they chose the cover they did.

Who wrote it? Ask each student to write one paragraph about something that is important to him or her—you might write one as well—but tell them not to put their name on it. Then read all or a sampling of the paragraphs aloud, to see if students can guess each paragraph's author. Explain that very little is known about the author of *Sir Gawain and the Green Knight*, except what has been conjectured from the poem itself. You might want to discuss books students are currently reading and ask what they can guess about the author based on the book. Students can then research the author to find out how accurate their guesses were.

The Three Estates (Reproducible #1): Ask students to go back to this reproducible (page 17) and place the names of the main characters from this play in their proper estates.

In Other Words (Reproducible #3): In this activity, students will do a word search to find the modern English word for some Middle English words. Those who find all the words will get a bonus—a piece of trivia about the legend of King Arthur. (Depending on the level of your students, you may want to provide students with the list of modern English words.)

Answers: 1-armorer, 2-clattering, 3-cousin, 4-deep, 5-dimple, 6-medicine, 7-here, 8-no, 9-nozzle, 10-rushed, 11-fool, 12-stream, 13-you, 14-there, **Bonus**-*Excalibur* is the name of King Arthur's magic sword.

Further Reading

The Challenge of the Green Knight by Ian Serrailler (Walck, 1967).

Name _____

In Other Words...

Look at the list of words below. Do they look familiar? They might, since they are in Middle English—the language from which our modern English developed. Find and circle the modern English word that means the same thing as each Middle English word in the word box. (Words can go up and down or across. No word completely overlaps another word.) Then write the modern English words on the lines. (You'll find clues for a few words.)

Middle English words

1. armoyer __ __ __ __ __ __
2. clatterande __ __ __ __ __ __ __ __ __ __
3. coz __ __ **u s** __ __
4. depe __ __ __ __
5. dimpul __ __ __ __ __ __
6. fisyk **m** __ **d** __ __ __ __ __
7. hither __ __ **r** __

8. nay __ __
9. nozle __ __ __ __ __ __
10. rusched __ __ __ __ __ __ __
11. simpkin **f** __ __ __
12. streem __ __ __ __ __ __
13. thee __ __ **u**
14. thither __ __ __ __ __ __

Word Box

C	L	A	T	T	E	R	I	N	G
O	Y	O	U	I	S	U	T	O	H
U	E	S	N	A	M	S	E	O	D
S	F	T	K	F	I	H	E	R	E
I	A	R	M	O	R	E	R	N	E
N	G	E	A	O	R	D	T	H	P
U	R	A	S	L	T	H	E	R	E
D	I	M	P	L	E	M	A	G	I
C	S	N	O	Z	Z	L	E	W	O
R	D	M	E	D	I	C	I	N	E

Bonus:
When you are done, write the remaining letters on the lines below to answer the question:

What is Excalibur?

Excalibur __ __ __ __ __ __ __ __ __ __ __ __ __ __ __ __

__ __ __ __ __ __ __ , __ __ __ __ __ __ __ __ __ __ __ __ .

READ ALOUD PLAYS: SIR GAWAIN AND THE GREEN KNIGHT
Scholastic Professional Books, 1998